dave dances . . .

life, love and art inspired by the music

of the dave matthews band

Dave Dances...life, love and art inspired by the music of the dave matthews band

www.LJMSArt.com

Design by Lynda Jo Mykkanen Sokolowski

Published by LJMS Art, New York

Library of Congress Control Number: 2007909563

ISBN -13: 978-0-9800379-1-3
ISBN -10: 0-9800379-1-3

Printed in China

First Edition: March 2008

10 9 8 7 6 5 4 3 2

dave dances

Lynda Jo Mykkanen Sokolowski

life, love and art inspired by the music

of the dave matthews band

for ben (old) (bald) & (baby)

Don't lose the dreams inside your head

I can't believe that we would lie in graves
Wondering if we had spent our living days well
I can't believe that we would lie in graves
Wondering what we might of been

\- DAVID J. MATTHEWS

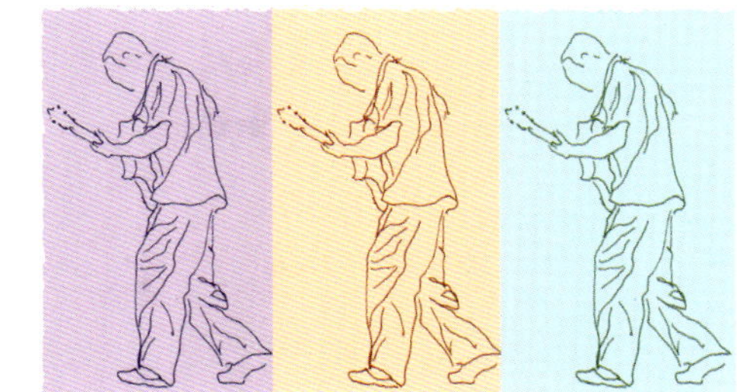

table of contents

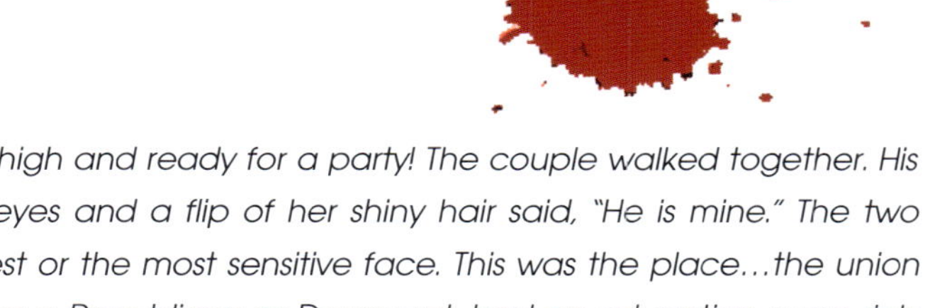

A few notes about "Dave Dances"

She hobbled in…legs tired…eyes wrinkled…a bit worn from life. He flew in…all tattooed and high and ready for a party! The couple walked together. His cargo shorts and Guinness tee bespoke his age…his time…his place. Her cute tank, sexy eyes and a flip of her shiny hair said, "He is mine." The two young girls literally sparkled in…all giggles and sweetness…searching the crowd for the cutest or the most sensitive face. This was the place…the union of the many. Differences were cast aside for one short time. It didn't matter whether you were a Republican or Democrat, had an education, were rich or poor, old or young, sick, lonely, a jerk…nothing mattered. This was the body working as one. This was a Dave Matthews Band concert. Soon the music would start, then the smiles and the dancing and for just a short time, all would be right with the world…

Sometimes things come to you blown in on a tornado - rough and fast and then other times, things unfold like a flower opening, petal by petal. This book has been like the latter - gentle and soft, slow and complex. It began for me a little over 2 years ago. As usual, the ride home from my son's house was always long...and boring. I missed him. We had moved. He had stayed. I missed my old home but I didn't know yet that today would be different. Today I would hear the perfect words sang just to me.... just for me.

> *I can't believe that we would lie in our graves*
> *Wondering if we had spent our living days well*
> *I can't believe that we would lie in our graves*
> *Dreaming of things that we might have been…could have been.*

The music came from the cd that my son had just given me. He would always have a new version of "#41" or the very best "Bartender" ...always a surprise for the long ride home. I heard those words and knew that this was sung just for me. And so I began to paint…

As I painted, the stories began to come. The very first story that I was told was Todd's story for Josh. Then came Antoinette's story for Abigail. Gentle stories of sadness, joy and redemption started to come to me as requests for various paintings were made. I had always been moved by the lyrics that Dave wrote...perceptive, intuitive, able to reach in and touch my heart and soul but now I was hearing stories of the affect of his music on others. I knew this was something that I wanted to share not only with the band but also with the people who made up these fans.

This "unwitting prophet"(as my friend Tim called Dave) was unique. This band was unique. This was far reaching. To me, this was important. There were other musicians who have impacted culture. Certainly, the Beatles. Bob Dylan, Nirvana – they all have played an important role in our musical atmosphere but who went beyond that? Who actually affected the philosophy of living and of love in such a specific way? It was there before my eyes in the form of these "love letters" to the band that sang of a world of celebration, of the joy & pain of life, of thankfulness, of passion, of finding the place where we all connect.... of that place that lies somewhere between the band playing on a stage on a beautiful summer night and that moon that shines so brightly...

I have left these stories very much as they were originally written. I have edited very little. It has been important to me from the beginning that these stories were told in each person's individual voice - not mine. The photos belong to the fans. "Grace Is Gone", "Dancing Nancies", "Butterfly", "Two Step" - all the music – these are each Dave's "dances" - each perhaps that little ode to life that make his feet dance a bit disfunctionallly and the words and feelings soar in a way that becomes magic.

So why would you care
To get out of this place
You and me and all our friends
Such a happy human race
'Cause we're tripping Billies.

I have learned a lot. I have learned that every voice is important, that joy comes in many forms, that music heals, and that music sometimes can make the memory of the pain too much. But what I understand best is that this fantastic band unites. It gives voice to every human emotion. I have read stories of all types and moods and places and dreams and never have I seen a group of people who speak kindness, believe in joy, live friendship, and maybe even whisper..."The world CAN be a better place!"

Lynda

And, yes! I just might get a tattoo!

1 warehouse

"Keep all your sights on.
The black cat changing colors.
I can walk under ladders.
And swim as the tides choose to turn me."

Black Cat
Black Cat
Black Cat
Black Cat
Black Cat
I can walk under ladders
Shut up I'm thinking

03.06

ware·house: \ˈwer-ˈhau̇s\
Function: *noun*
Date: 14th century:
1: a structure or room for the storage of merchandise or commodities

"This I admit
Taste so good,
Hard to believe an end to it
Smell touch feel
How could this rhythm ever quit?
Bags packed on a plane
Hopefully to heaven."

Clockwise from top: Stephen, Carly, Adam, Troy, Tiffany, Chris, Julie, Kelly

It was the summer of 2005 at Saratoga Performing Arts Center in Saratoga, New York. The venue is an amphitheater...therefore it has an outdoor (grass) and indoor area. My friends and I were on the grass. It happened to be a realllly rainy night, it basically felt like a monsoon. Near the railing to the inside section there was a group of people holding a pool tarp over there heads (about 10-15 people). My friend Harrison and I were not happy about this because it was obstructing our view of the show so we proceeded to go over and rip the tarp from them. Little did we know, the 10-15 people were actually 10-15 huge football looking type people. They were not happy at all.

They got in our face and wanted to fight.

As soon as this happened, about 20-25 people from the c'owd grabbed our shirts from behind and pulled us behind them and said to the jock guys "what are you gonna do now?" This of course was AWESOME. So Harrison and I then decided to lay the tarp on the slope of the grass and use it as a slip and slide. Then tons of people started to join in. According to the security guard (who happened to look about 75 years old and said he'd been working at the park for 20 years) it was the first slip and slide he's ever seen at a show there.

This experience simply added to how much I love this band.
What other concert would you see a bunch of people angry one minute and ripping there shirts off and sliding down a hill the next??

Brian Maher

"Hey reckless mind Don't throw away your playful beginning..."

Dave Matthews Band

Band photos by David Adam Beloff

It's September of 2006. I have never been to a Dave Matthews Band concert!

The last concert I'd gone to was the Jackson 5 back in 1970 something!

Well, this time I was one of only 10 African-Americans in the entire venue and felt a little strange about being there – not to mention the fact that I'd come alone. It's not easy going any place alone. I was feeling kind of out of place, but before I knew it people were talking to me, some people drank with me, others fed me, People danced with me and helped me celebrate my wonderful night out with Dave & the boyz. Inclusive! Joyful! Awesome!

"Thank you! Just in a moment I'm gonna be joined by all my friends up here and then we're gonna funk it hard until midnight and then a little afterwards. So we hope you all stay. Hope that your bar-hopping doesn't necessarily drag you away. You could hop away then hop back or just pretend you hopped away and not hop away at all."

-- David J. Matthews

03.17.93 The Floodzone - Richmond, VA

D is for
DAVE
16821
DAVE MATTHEWS
THE GORGE
GEORGE, WA
2006
summer tour
RESERVED SEATS Inc.
County Tax
X4 SEC B
12 Row
Dave is GORGES
RED EYED
EH HEE!!
GORGE '07
dmb
HONK 4 DMB
41

cartwheel

When I attend a DMB show, I usually don't get very excited until right before the show starts. Reason is I have a million things going on in my head with work and a phone that never stops ringing. To signal to myself and everyone else that I am ready to focus on ME and the show and to have fun - I do a cartwhee!! Crazy but that is when nothing else matters! Kind of a thing I have and maybe need to keep me from going crazy.

Chelsea

It was the summer tour, the Band was touring in Virginia Beach, and me and my mom had great third row seats. The "Stand Up" album had recently come out, and my most favorite song on the album was "Stolen Away on 55st and 3rd". It was so good, I decided to make a homemade shirt saying "Steal Me Away" on it. I was so excited to wear it to the show, hoping it would bring me luck and they would play it. Well, after a long beautiful show, there was no sign of them playing my song. A little disappointed, but certainly not upset since the show was spectacular, my mom and I waited for the Band to come back on stage to perform the encore. As the members walked back on stage, accompanying Dave was a chair. My mom and I had no idea what he would play sitting down. But, to my surprise, Dave Matthews himself, just before he was seated, gave me a point to acknowledge my shirt, and started to play the infamous song! Everyone looked at me and screamed and clapped, as I looked around oblivious that Dave Matthews had just pointed directly at me. My eyes filled up with tears and I let the music embrace me while I closed my eyes and just absorbed the moment. The shirt hasn't been washed since, and it's now famously hung on my wall.

Now when everyone asks about it, I have an amazing story to tell. :)

Chelsea Bland
15 years old
Virginia Beach, VA

"Shotgun" by Chelsea

"Upside Down?" by Chelsea

painted by the most talented Chelsea Bland

Amy's bulletin board

Friends we made at shows!

I love to stay here . . .

Photo by Jesse DeVries

I have been to shows far into the double digits but when the house lights go out and you know that the guys are getting ready to take the stage, I still get that jittery butterfly feeling in my stomach EVERY single time. Then I catch my first glimpse of them walking out on stage. I get goosebumps and chills. And when I hear the crowd singing along, it is just absolutely magical to be a part of this sea of love.

Ceason 

THE WAREHOUSE

So it's early on a Monday morning and someone said to me that if you want to be a good writer you have to write a lot. Someone also said to me once that if you don't want to go to jail you'll put your pants back on, and that worked out well so we'll see how this goes. So this morning how I woke up may have given me a hint that I have a huge obsessive-compulsive disorder when it comes to DMB. I was off in dreamland and there were these two girls in a major pillow fight and they had these Catholic schoolgirl outfits on...let me stop right now 'cause that dream really has no bearing on the story. Anywhosel, so I was dreaming and I heard someone say "Dave Matthews" and I woke up instantly. Now this was one of those times where you wake up and you aren't for sure whether you heard someone say Dave Matthews or you just thought you did, but I looked at the T.V. and this guy was starting to play a song on the guitar and I think he said that some people said that he played songs like Jack Johnson or Dave Matthews. So apparently if there is a tornado coming I will be blown away unless anyone says "Dave Matthews" then I will wake right up and be ready to go. Almost like a ninja. (If by "ninja" you mean someone who wakes up very slowly, scratches his balls a lot and wears a shirt that says "Where's the beef?"). That is how I woke up this morning.

So yesterday I'm just farting around on the computer before work and I went to check in at the Warehouse website to see when my tickets for Alpine were coming in. I get to the shipping screen for the address. Apparently, Murphy (of Murphy's Law fame) had kicked me right in the scrotum one more time. Now in all the towns and cities that I have ever lived, the address has been like 1435 Grey St. or 4136 Townsquare Blvd. But now my address starts with 16013. That is just the first part of it. I get tired just writing that part, so in any event when I changed my address I accidentally put 16301. And for the Warehouse I needed to change my address for shipping the tickets by August 28th. Today was September 3rd. As I came to this realization, panic set in. Real actual panic. Like me yelling "s--t, b--ls, and c--------r" all in the same sentence. And then walking around the room sweating saying things like "We have a Code 4". And I gotta be honest with you, I don't even know what a Code 4 is. So I tried to call the Warehouse, but I forgot that it is a holiday weekend and most likely nobody would be there until Tuesday. Which is the 4th, and my tickets aren't supposed to ship out until the 11th. So I emailed them and let them know what was up and that I was waiting to hear back. But the nice thing is that I posted a bulletin on myspace asking if anyone had this problem before, and was relieved to find out that it's not too big of a problem and it would most likely be fixed. So I really gotta say, DMB fans come through again. Otherwise yesterday my actions at work would have been weird. I explained my situation to every single person that came through my line and asked them what they thought would happen and then marked their answer down on a sheet. Then I looked at it at the end of the day and compared everyone's answers. That's kinda how I am sometimes...how I make decisions. Either that or I figured I could camp out in front of the person's house whose address I accidentally put down. That may get kinda odd for them. Especially when I built a bonfire and tracked and hunted "Sparky" (their dog) for food. But Sparky would be delicious and everyone would have a good laugh about it the end. 'Cause in my world everything ends happily and strangely enough there are always two girls dressed up in Catholic schoolgirl outfits pillow fighting.

The End

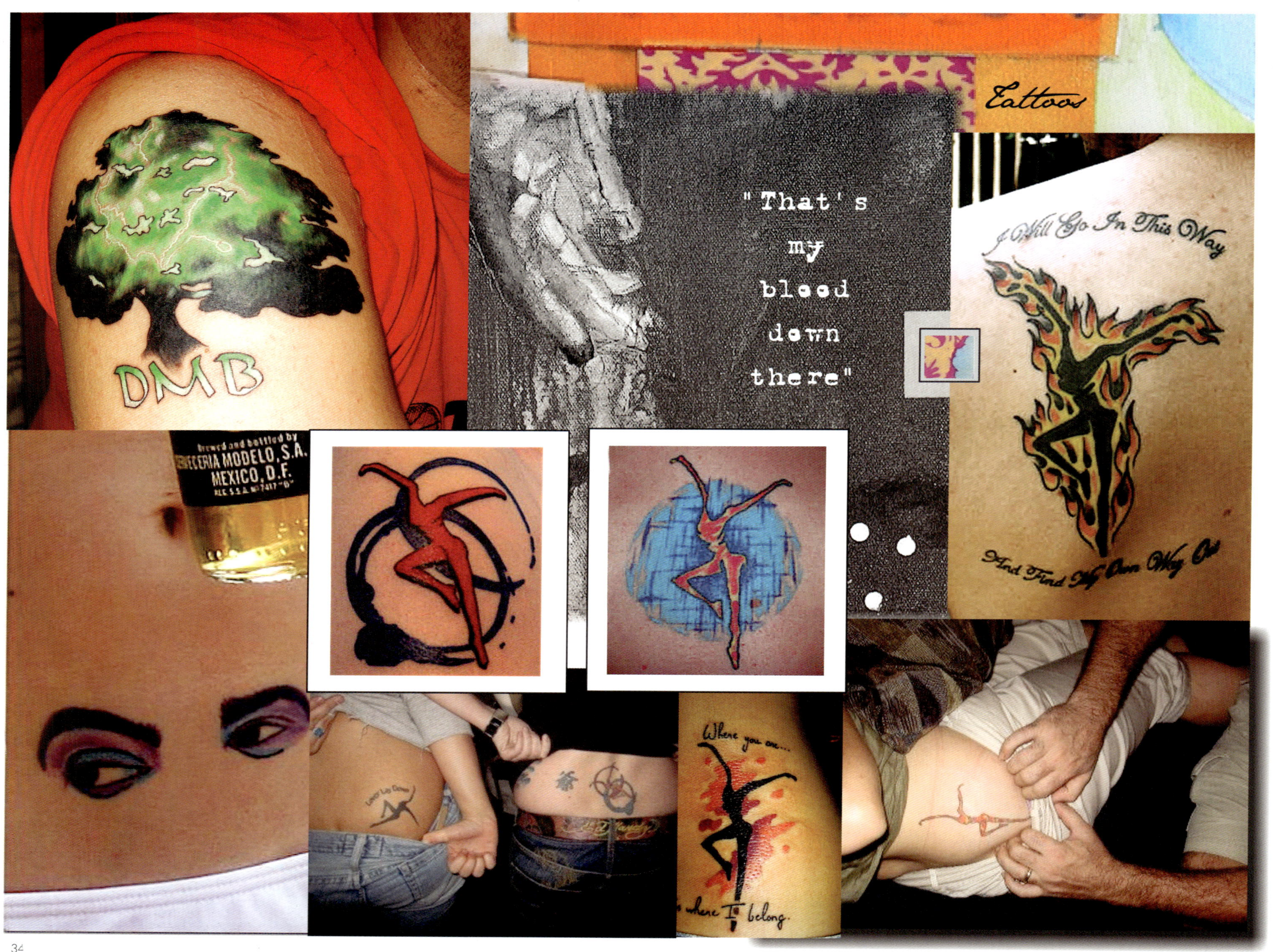
DMB
Brewed and bottled by
MODELO, S.A.
MEXICO, D.F.
Tattoos
"That's my blood down there"
I Will Go In This Way
And Find My Own Way Out
Where you are...
where I belong

England's #1 DMB fan –
Paul from Liverpool –
at the home of
the Beatles!
CAVERN
club
DAVE MATTHEWS BAND

When you think about it, it's not easy to name that many front men
(or any men for that matter) that have the voice, the talent, the following,
and that unexplainable appeal that just makes us sit like kids
with wide eyes on Christmas any time he or his music is present.
Who else could mess up the words, play a wrong chord
and have a hoarse crack of the voice
without making the song sound bad???

Church for the musical soul!!!

(How many talents and bitchin' quirks can one guy have???)

 Tim

My love I love to stay here
In the warehouse . . .

2 butterfly

"You are like a butterfly.
A caterpillar's dream to fly"

You are like
a butterfly
A Caterpillars
dream to fly
So bust out of
this old cocoon

01.06

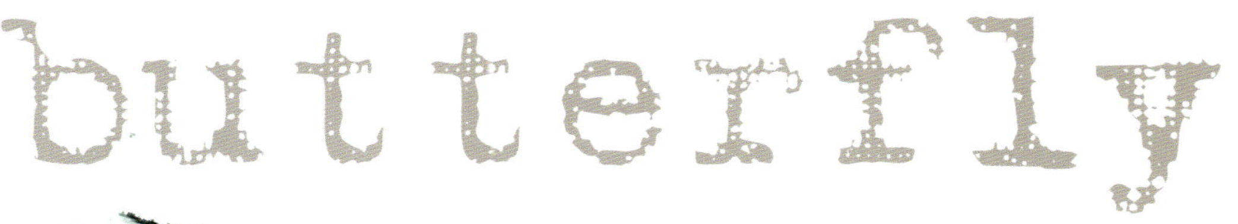

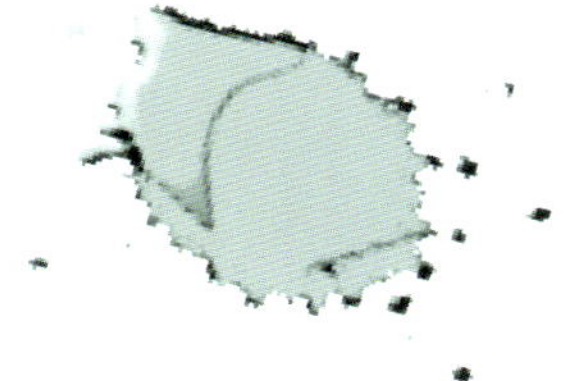

chrys·a·lis : \ˈkri-sə-ləs\
Function: *noun*
plural **chry·sal·i·des** \kri-ˈsa-lə-ˌdēz\
or **chrys·a·lis·es** Date:1601
1 a: a pupa of a butterfly; *broadly* : an insect pupa **b:** the enclosing case or covering of a pupa **2:** a protecting covering : a sheltered state or stage of being or growth

"You are like a butterfly
A caterpillar's dream to fly
Bust out of this old cocoon
Dry your wings off, butterfly..."

Dear Dave and Band,

Your music has inspired and transformed our lives for years. My wife, friends and I have a special connection through your music. The emotion you pour into each song is felt by us all and it has made for some great memories and experiences. Please let me share with you one of these unforgettable experiences.

My younger brother Joshua died on August 29th at the age of 30. He was a musician, biologist and an environmentalist...one of his interests was butterflies and he has used them as symbolism in his music and art. When asked why, he had said that a butterfly, to him, represented transformation of the soul, spiritual awakening and freedom. At his funeral, under a clear blue northern Michigan sky, we released Monarch butterflies in his honor. No words can describe how much we miss him. Ironically, the night before he died, my wife, kids and I were watching "Because of Winn-Dixie" and it was the first time we had heard your song "Butterfly" and smiling, we all remarked that Josh would like this.

Fast forwarding ahead, after he died I was so very sad and each day searched for some sign or connection that he was still with us in spirit but dissappointedly came up empty handed.

My wife and I went to Red Rocks all four nights to see you and the band. (we're medical professionals, parents AND we still find the time to see you all summer long!) It could have been the combination of beautiful scenery, great times at hand, or alcohol (just kidding!) but on night three something magical happened.

As we were all jamming to the music, I suddenly started to withdrawl in my mind...thinking of my brother Joshua and I looked up at the stars. Still feeling the warm energy of the music and the crowd, I looked at my wife and said "God, I wish Josh could be here to share this awesome experience with us." As we both looked back up into the sky I said

"Give us a sign that you're with us, Josh."

The very next song you played was Butterfly, and as the first few notes were played, this surreal wind kicked up from the stage and blew up into the crowd. We stared at each other with sheer excitement and awe as goosebumps covered us. To me this event gave me a feeling of peace and closure to what I had been looking for over the last few weeks since his passing. I looked back up into that starry night sky with tears in my eyes and said "thank you." We will never forget that great moment.

Thank you VERY, very much for all your beautiful music and what it's done for our lives.

Peace & Love,

Todd and Tawny Richards

Rachael backstage at Raley Field
Sacramento, CA
2006

Photo by TriplLght Imaging

You are like a butterfly
A Catipillars dream to fly
So bust out of this old cocoon
And dry your wings off

Butterfly

JMac

Dave Matthews Band

*"Chrysalis is really hard to say in a song
especially if you've had
a couple of whiskies."*

-- David J. Matthews

Band photos by David Adam Beloff

Sam

Bitch teachers locked me in a room and i wasnt aloud to ~~that~~ have any Human contact for 3 days!

DMB!

alright. so i went to catholic school from kindergarten to 4th grade, i then went to public school for 2 years and my mom begged and pleaded the principal to get me back into the catholic school for 7th and 8th grade. she finally allowed it. and ever since i went there it was hell. they were after me. every little thing would do i got in trouble for. and im not one to let anyone walk all over me. so i would talk back and be disrespectful which just dug a deeper hole. now, 7th grade wasnt as bad as 8th. 8th grade, i fell into a huge depression… i was getting in so much trouble at school. it got to the point …

where i wouldn't even do things and i got in trouble. of course i would come home and tell my parents and they would just be like okay okay, you have to go to school. because of course they dont know what goes on in school. so i just kept falling and falling so depressed. it felt like i had no one. i decided i wanted to end my life, i had written a suicide note. explaining everything and why i chose that. and one night i was so angry because my parents were making me go to school knowing that i had in schcol suspension the next day, in which the bitch teachers locked me in a room and i wasnt aloud to have any human contact with anyone the entire school day. for 3 days. that night i was so fed up i went in my room got out my suicide not threw it in my moms face and shut my door. It broke my parents hearts. i had always been a fan of dave's music. just because i kinda grew up around it, my brothers are musicians so they know good music. so i was always listening to a little dmb hear and there. but 8th grade it really sparked. i was listening to them non stop. i would take dave's words and they felt so real it felt like it was me he was talking to. dave completely changed my mind on my suicide. He complete turned my life around. and the one line that really stuck out to me was "dark clouds may hang on me sometimes but ill work it out" from dancing nancies. so yes. he has inspired me so much. i am a complete different person as i was last year. completey different. you know, i realize how precious life is. i am since now in counseling. And my counsler is actually a dave fan, so we talk a lot about him which also helps me out a lot. I am since now in 9th grade and I am homeschooled because of the school I was in. Being homeschooled has allowed me to listen to dave more often and it also has allowed me to find me, and figure out who I am. Since this year, my mom has told me so many times I am mature for my age, and it makes me feel good because you know who I owe it to? Dave. Everything for him. He is my hero. He saved me. if it wasnt for him and his inspiring music i wouldnt have changed my mind. i wouldnt have completely turned my life around. I owe dave my life, and I cant wait until that day I get to meet him and let him know, that if I wasn't for him I wouldn't be here right now.

Sam

15 years old

Pottstown, PA.

A note from Lynda:

"Sam hasn't got to meet Dave yet but thanks to her brother, Nick, Dave called her while he swam in the Atlantic this summer!" (2007)

Band photos by David Adam Beloff

Dry your tears away, butterfly
Go ahead, and fly

My story is kind of sad but it doesn't end that way. In 2001 my husband committed suicide in front of me and our year old daughter. At that moment I felt the world just stopped and that was all I could think about. The morning of his funeral I was listening to the radio and a DMB song came on. (Sorry can't recall what song) My heart just skipped a beat. The weeks went by and I thought nothing of it. In December a friend and I went the see the band at Madison Square Garden, I think I saw maybe two songs without tears. I was the music and love was all around me and I could just feel the hurt and pain going away. It was just for a few hours but it felt so, so good. I was now a fan reborn. I had always liked the music but never as much as after that night, As Dave says "what you got lay it down on me". I do every chance I get. Now I'm remarried and have a new child (his initials are JTR). It may be corny but thanks to the music and love that surrounds the band, I was brought back from a very, very bad place and given back my rose colored glasses! And I am ever so grateful for them. I don't get to see as many shows as I would like. Motherhood comes first for me but when I do go it's always as soul cleansing as that magical night long ago at the Garden.

JTR

Forever a DMB fan
Erica Rahoche
New Jersey

Artie

My name is Artie and this is my Dave Matthews Band story. In December of 2005 part of my life changed in a dramatic way. My son, Artie Jr. had a serious drug addiction and was in a drug rehab program here in NY. This situation had been tearing me apart for a couple of years and even though he was in treatment and doing pretty well, it seemed like I had lost my beautiful 25-year-old son forever. The laughter and big smile seemed permanently erased from his handsome face, I always felt this underlying feeling that he'd much rather be "high" than to be with me. He always had somewhere else to be or something to do that never once included me. The pain in my heart was unbearable and I finally, after some real heavy soul searching, began to think I should give up and try and move on in my life without him.

A few years prior to this, Artie Jr. had become a huge DMB fan and began attending shows all around the Tri-State area . I had listened to a little DMB before but my son kept having me listen to different cds and in no time I became a major "Dave" fan.

I got tickets for the December 10, 2005 Madison Square Garden concert on Ebay. I wanted these tickets and paid over $600 and I was hoping that there was even a slight chance that I could take my son to this show even though I knew the people in the rehab center probably would not let him go. I wanted this to be the most fun Christmas gift my son had received in a long time and I wanted to share that night with him...

In some way I felt that this would be my last chance in this life to find the son I lost.

Miraculously they let him attend the show and gave him a curfew that was reasonable. We were going to our first Dave Matthews show as father and son!

After taking the train to NYC we arrived at Penn Station and you could actually feel the excitement in the air as we were going up the stairs from Penn Station to The Garden. While going up the stairs I felt a "shift", a "crack" in my right hip and pain shot through my hip and down my right leg, I was "frozen", I could not move at that moment. I stood on those steps and tried to figure out how I would get up these remaining steep steps until we got to the escalator. I didn't want this night ruined. I summoned whatever strength I could muster to get up those steps and I did. My son knew something was wrong, he had a concerned look on his face but I assured him I was okay... Our seats were great - on the floor very close to the sound board. We were here at our first DMB show together! My son was smiling as wide as I'd seen him smile in a very long time. His eyes were sparkling and he seemed relaxed which was in complete contrast to what had become his normal nervousness.

The show began and it was fantastic! The set list was unbelievcble from the first song to the last and it seemed like the band knew this night was special for us. I watched from the corner of my eye as the band played "#41" which is my son's favorite song (He has a large #41 tattoo on his forearm) and he was dancing and smiling and raising his arms in the air and I began to cry because I had seen him so sad and so lost for so long and at this moment I saw that he could still experience "joy" despite his addiction nightmare... My leg was hurting so bad that I stood on one leg for the entire show and since my son had stood from the opening song to the last, I was able to get away with it and not give myself away. Tonight was Artie Jr.'s night and nothing was going to change that fact. When the show was over we were both exhausted, the encore that night was incredible and we sang and cheered so much that our voices were gone. It was a night to remember. I knew neither of us would ever forget it.

I went to the Doctor the next day and was diagnosed with a hip fracture. The bone had actually broke off from the torque caused by the steep steps and was floating inside my leg causing severe pain and other collateral damage. I had surgery and recovered over the next six months.

When my son heard about the fracture to my leg he was felt terrible. He came to visit me at home a few days later. When I went to the bathroom, he said he was going outside to smoke a cigarette. When I looked for him through the curtains I saw he was crying and I knew he was crying for me.......And it was then that I realized ...he was back! This was the kid I remembered! I knew my son and he would not cry in front of me if he was crying about me. This was the signal I had been looking for. This showed me something I had not seen in a very long time.

I'm happy to say that my son is no longer in treatment for his drug addiction. He is now a Drug and Alchohol Rebab counselor in Phoenix House helping young adults who are battling substance abuse problems. He plans on furthering his education in this field and making this his career. I am so proud of him. Words cannot describe how I feel.

The Dave Matthews Band helped a father and son who were as close as can be, then got separated by heartbreaking circumstances, get back together and re-establish their lifelong bond as father and son, buddies, music fans and friends. I suppose many people will say "What does the DMB really have to do with this story?" My answer would be this: They were a catalyst. They were the "common ground"- a place to start...

Artie
Philadelphis, PA.

Band photos by David Adam Beloff

The rain had just stopped.

The clouds lifted and

through the gray was

the sky, so blue...

It was then that he put

his hand on my cheek

and said.

"You know,

you are like a butterfly"

. . . and I was!

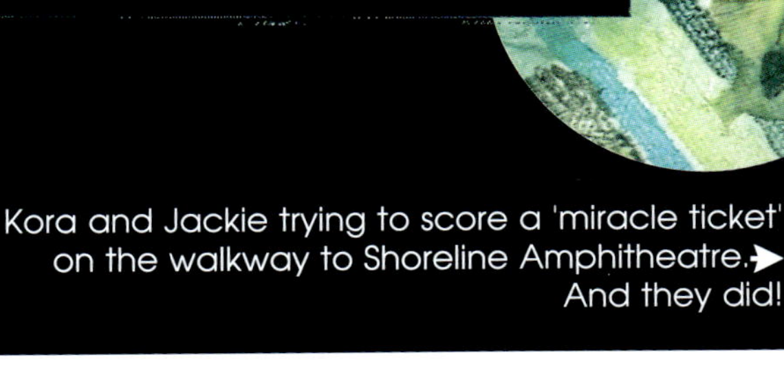

Megan

Kora and Jackie trying to score a 'miracle ticket'
on the walkway to Shoreline Amphitheatre.➤
And they did!

3
dancing nancies

"I am who I am who I am who am I?
Requesting some enlightenment
Could I have been anyone other
than me?"

01.06

dancing nancy: \'dan(t)s-ing nan(t)-sE\
Function:*noun*
Date:19th century:
1: a dancing prostitue (European)
2: a transvestite prostitute

"Could I have been
A parking lot attendant?
Could I have been
A millionaire in Bel Air?
Could I have been lost
somewhere in Paris?
Could I have been
Your little brother?
Could I have been
Anyone other than me?"

Sara

It started when I was in middle school...
the years every teenager dreads.
You know, the years when your body starts to change. You get made fun of because of it, blah blah blah. Well, this was the beginning, for me, of a sickness that I could not control. When I got to high school, I was okay, submerging myself in my school's marching band surrounded by "friends", but really escaping those years with only one truly good friend. Depression is something talked about more commonly lately, with it affecting so many people around us.

Many people are put on meds,
Others use other things to take away the pain.
Mine was music.

It was my freshman year of high school, and I was going through alot....emotionally. I was anti-social, crying every night, not knowing why and wondering what was wrong with me. I was n a depression and I didn't even know it. The type of depression where you simply could not bring yourself to raise a finger to dc anything for yourself or for anyone. One warm, August evening, I decided to escape to my bedroom (my sanctuary, to escape my demons). My parents' house backed up to a place called Meadowbrook Music Festival, Living in Rochester Hills, Michigan fɔr so long, it was a summer ritual of mine to listen to the concerts that went on at the venue from my own backyard. Well, on this ɔarticular night in August, I could hear, dancing among the night air, a violin, a guitar, drums and bass with the notes of a saxophcne and a raspy, fun loving voice riding behind the breeze. It took me a second to remember that the Dave Matthews Band were in town and playing a concert that very night at Meadowbrook!

So, in my bedroom, I was...curtains open (my bedroom window faced the backyard, towards the venue) head resting on my arms on my windowsill...I listened...to the whole concert. After hearing "Exodus" and "Ants Marching", I remember thinking that this was the beginning of a beautiful friendship. My high scool years went by fast, with my Senior year approaching and me going to Seattle as a graduation gift from my best friend's father. Before I left for my trip, I picked up "Before These Crowded Streets". This CD was a lifesaver...literally. After moving out of my parents' house (my father and I clashed then...we are okay now that I am not at home anymore) I fell into a deeper depression. One evening, after a big fight with a "friend" of mine (I say friend in quotes because these are people who ended up just bringing me more down than up in my life) I went home, to my grandparents whom I was living with at the time, and proceeded to try and take my own life. That night was a blur because I was trying to reach out to someone and it seemed like no one cared...or so I thought. I ended up, after that night, being put through two weeks of day hospital to get me back on my feet. During that time, I used Dave Matthews Band's music to heal myself. The music helped me to see things about myself, and my life that seemed to make things click. Listening to this music and listening to these lyrics made me believe everything was going to be 'okay, okay, okay...'. I couldn't "burn the day away"...I had to live for myself and for everyone I loved because "at what point could there be troubling...head down, wondering what would become of me..."

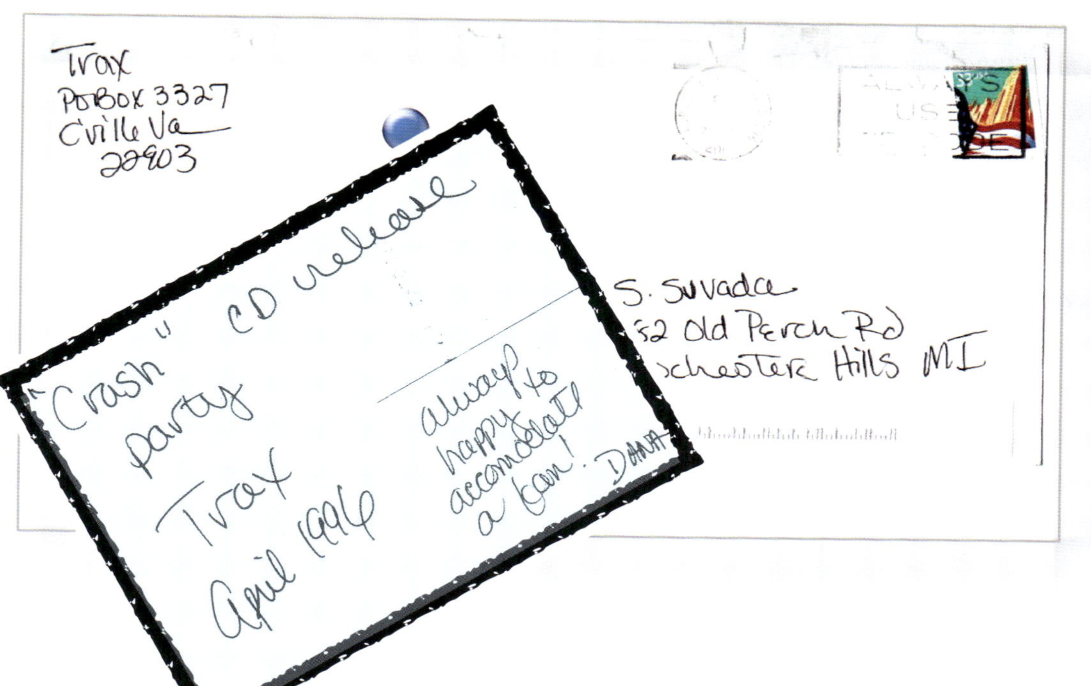

Rockin' Comerica

The Oakland Press/PAULA ARTMAN

Dave Matthews, leader of the Dave Matthews Band, performs before a sold-out crowd at Comerica Park. It was the first concert at the new home of the Detroit Tigers, and 43,822 fans were there to witness the landmark show. For a review of the concert, see **Page A-9.**

This song, "Pig", guides my life...daily...monthly...yearly.

I have been through so much heartache. Now for once in my life, I can say that life is the most important thing to me and that I want to live to see the day that I can tell Dave Matthews "Thank you". From the bottom of my heart. For making a girl like me really see that life was truly worth living. Music not only heals the depths of our souls, but makes us hunger for life. I have seen DMB 17 times...and I am still going....I need to reach my goal. Dave...if you are out there somewhere reading this...thank you....

Every word is from my heart.

Sara
1998

Sara
27 years old
Rochester, MI

Sing and dance I'll play for you tonight
The thrill of it all
Dark clouds may hang on me sometimes
But I'll work it out

Photo by David Adam Beloff

Laurie

I had been writing songs for years without an instrument and was too afraid to even touch a guitar. I was sure I could never play. 3 months ago I met Dave Matthews and it changed my life. I had this uncontrollable need to start teaching myself and it's like I've unleashed this world of power, this passion I didn't know I had. I feel like I've woken up. Now I'm writing song after song with my guitar (incredible) and I have since written a song about the man himself. I've just submitted my material to the casting for a new MTV reality series about singer/songwriters. I would have never been able to do that without Dave and his music and immeasurable influence in my world.

Mad Hatter he say,
Dance like me.
C'mon Baby,
it's your chance.
Be Free.
Come and dance with me
you look so fine
in the dripping colors,
in the slipping time'
And it's deep,
this heavy high.
It's deep,
this you and I

"I have a message from Bill who is in the 7th row. This message is a request. It says DAVE - PLEASE play "Lover Lay Down" because if you play that, I will get laid by my girlfriend, Jill." (Then Dave says,) "Hey Bill, I wrote the damn song, if anything, Jill and I should be getting it on tonight!"

- David J. Matthews

01.20.07 Hass Auditorium (Bloomsburg University) - Bloomsburg, PA

sweet
caroline
FENWAY
DMB
41
NO PARKING

"What's the use in worrying,
What's the use in hurrying
Turn, turn we almost become dizzy"

The night was pure wonder!

The music became me . . .

like blood through my veins . . .

like a spirit of joy

or redemption

or flight.

I had become part of

the dance

where love swings

and stars light the sky forever . . .

Randall's Island 2006

4
grace is gone

"Neon shines through smoky eyes tonight
It's 2 am - I'm drunk again
it's heavy on my mind"

03.06

grace is gone

grace: \'gras\
Function:*noun*
Date:12th century:
1 a: unmerited divine assistance given humans for their regeneration or sanctification**2 a: approval, favor** <stayed in his good *graces*> **b:** *archaic* **: mercy, pardon.**

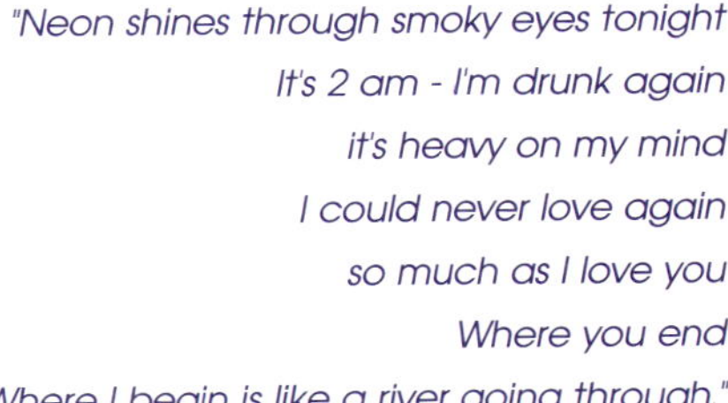

"Neon shines through smoky eyes tonight
It's 2 am - I'm drunk again
it's heavy on my mind
I could never love again
so much as I love you
Where you end
Where I begin is like a river going through."

Back in the summer of 1998 my best friend asked me if I wanted to go to a Dave Matthews Band concert. I had heard of them and was always up for good time so I figured why not? Who would have known after seeing DMB for the first time in July of 1998 that it would lead to so many good times and a few bad over the next 9 years?

One show and I was hooked. Luckily for us we ran into some friends with extra tickets for the following night. The next day at work I heard for the first time of many to come, "Why are you going to see them two nights in a row?" I already knew that you had to see them any chance you could. Every show is different and you never knew when you'd hear that one song that will make you wanna dance or cry. There have been so many great times over the last nine years listening to DMB. So many shows in Camden and Philly...an incredible day and night in Central Park...tailgating in Hershey... freezing cold night in State College... Madison Square Garden...once with James Brown and another with confetti...every DMB fan's ultimate trip to the Gorge - an absolutely beautiful place...Randall's Island...the last show with a great friend. Over 40 shows and still counting.

The thing about DMB's music is it moves me. There is a song for just about every emotion I can think of. If I'm in a great mood and wanna have fun, pop in "Warehouse". If I need inspiration, "Bartender", "Dancing Nancies" or "Ants Marching" always seems to get me pumped up. Dave's words define time and mark moments in our lives.

Maybe I wasn't the best husband but I left my pregnant wife at home that first July night in 1998. She didn't know too much about DMB at the time and wasn't a woman that was big into crowds. Amy was a petite blond and felt a little nervous around so many people. Shortly after those two concerts she became as big a fan of DMB as I was. She pretty much had to. Looking back it seems like there was always DMB playing in my jeep whenever we drove anywhere. I'm sure that's where our son, Connor, got his love for DMB. He has been listening to it since he was in Amy's belly. Connor was born in early 1999. As a result of childbirth Amy had some problems with her heart. There were a few trying months but thankfully things worked out, Amy got better and eventually came home. Connor wasn't more than a couple months old and he already had his own DMB cd. I vividly remember Amy singing "Christmas Song" to him as a lullaby. Oh how I wish I would have recorded it. Life was good. Life was perfect.

"Eat, Drink and be Merry…for tomorrow we die." It is a simple line, never much thought about but as it turns out, so true. In one moment my life and so many people's lives around me changed forever. Three days shy of Connor's second birthday, Amy had a heart attack and slipped into a coma. One moment she was on the floor playing with Connor and then next she was gone.

Over the next few months as Amy lay lifeless, friends, family and people I didn't even know somehow managed to keep mine and Connor's life from crashing down all around us. I would sit with Amy in the hospital, just the two of us in the room together and we would listen to DMB together. I must have played "Christmas Song" dozens of times hoping that she would hear it and somehow wake up.

In late February DMB released "Everyday". I didn't exactly have time with a two year old and my wife in the hospital to go out and buy it. In a moment of great friendship that I will never forget, my best friend, the one who took me to that first concert, went out at midnight the day it was released, bought me a cd and left it on my jeep. When I saw it in the morning, I was overwhelmed. Such a small gesture meant so much.

April 22nd I was at the nursing home visiting Amy and needed some fresh air. I decided to take a little walk and sat down and saw the most beautiful sunset I've ever seen. Shortly after midnight, Amy passed away. I have had never felt so empty and alone as I did then.
This could not have happened. I should not lose my wife at such a young age and certainly Connor shouldn't lose his mom before he barely knew her.
Somehow my life went from perfect to falling apart.

Three things kept me going in the coming days, months and years. First, my friends and family are absolutely the best. The support they have all given me and Connor are what it is all about. Second, I made a promise to Amy that I would do whatever is necessary to make sure I am the best father I can possibly be for Connor. All I need to see is his beautiful smile and I can see her smiling from above. He is the best kid and more than I could have ever wished for. Even at three years old he would bring me tissues and give me a hug when I was having a tough time. Lastly, the music of the Dave Matthews Band has been a great help. In particular the song "Grace is Gone". Listening to that song was like listening to Dave sing my feelings. I don't think there is a word in that song that didn't explain how I felt. It is such a beautiful song about the loss of love.
For a long time I struggled with the loss of Amy.
It takes time, pain and a little hope to get through losing a loved one.

"Grace is Gone" will always have a special place in my heart just as Amy always will.

Losing the one person that you love like no other and knows you like nobody else is never easy but the music of Dave Matthews Band has been there for me to make life just a little easier and much more fun.

Eat Drink and be Merry.....
I'll always love you Amy

Michael

➔ *Today, Connor is a beautiful, happy 9 year old boy.*

"Take my eyes take my heart I need them no more
If never again they fall upon the one I so adore."

Terry

I came to the Dave Matthews Band late in life. It was 1996 and I was 50 years old. While riding with a friend, I got to hear the "Crash" album. I immediately fell in love with this album and the band who recorded it. Little did I realize how important they would become in my life.
In the 1980s my mother became mentally ill, suffering from bi-polar disease. My father had heart disease and it was a life threatening situation. There was nothing that could be done for him. He and my mother lived alone and unbeknownst to their children he was doing his level best to hide the severity of her illness from everyone. Necr Easter in 1985, he discovered my mother with a plastic bag over her head. The stress was finally too much for him and he suffered a fatal heart attack. I was filled with guilt because I had been staying with them, to help him, and had chosen that particular night to go to my own home. At his funeral, my Mom was singing inappropriate songs, walking down the street in her bare feet, and even tried to stab me with a knife. How do you grieve in this situation?

Between my sister, my 2 brothers and myself we tried to help her as much as we could. Unfortunately, even severely mentally ill patients have rights that serve the purpose of allowing these people to continue to endanger themselves.
As the years went by, the rest of my family withdrew from her and left me to handle everything. I was losing time from work so i could help her, take her to doctor's appointments and be awakened in the middle of the night by phone calls of screaming and then hanging up. No matter what I did, and how many places I sought to get her help, it was to no avail. Eventually she was evicted from her apartment because she was so destructive. No matter how many times I took her to the hospital for failed suicide attempts, it was not enough for the mental health system to put her in the hospital, or to keep her there once she went. I managed to get her into a group home.
But I was still responsible for her doctor appointments, etc.
Over the years she made many more visits to the psychiatric ward of the hospitals, only to be released before any treatment helped. Finally, I had to do the hardest thing I had ever done in my life - go to court to have my mother committed.
She thought I was going to be her champion and I felt like I had betrayed her.
I wept for days. I became depressed, stressed, had trouble sleeping and came close to wanting to end my life.

This went on for years. I was never happy or calm.

Listening to the words, I felt as though I began to understand what my mother was going through.

Enter DMB.

As a result of the "Crash" album, I began to listen to their earlier recordings and loved them. I collected all their albums, read all I could about them and began to feel that they were my friends. I heard the song "Rhyme and Reason". It was like a miracle to me. Listening to the words, I felt as though I began to understand what my mother was going through. It was like peeking into her mind. The confusion, the pain, the feeling that she could not trust what she saw and heard, because she could not tell reality from madness. It helped me to get rid of my anger at her for not being able to live in the real world, and it made me much more sympathetic and understanding to her plight. It helped me to let go of the frustration of not being able to reach her or deal with her. I became a kinder more understanding daughter. This is not to say that I never was angry or frustrated again.

The song that most reached into my soul was "The Best of What's Around". I heard Dave saying "It seems your eyes are troubled. Care to share your time with me? Would you say you are feeling low and so, a good idea would be to get it off of your mind"

I felt my heart begin to expand with hope.

I felt this was written for me.

To this day those words prompt tears and a chill in me.

I put so much faith and hope in those words.

Photo by David Adam Beloff

" Seek Up" was also important in saving my life. Through that song, I gave myself permission to release my emotions instead of bottling them inside my self (they can't be kept at bay). I also suddenly knew that we can be forgiven for things we do.

Playing their songs released my mind and heart from the guilt, regret and pain I had felt for all those years. It helped me to deal more kindly with my mother. Dave knew what I had been feeling. He was writing about it, putting it into words and music. As the years go on, and I hear more and more of their music, I find still more songs that express how I feel about love, passion and life. DMB literally saved my life. They saved me from taking my life and they helped me to save those moments with my mother, when she was bright, charming and oh so cute, when she had those little windows of sanity. They were there to help me through her death, and to finally grieve for my Dad. I could never repay them for what they have done for me, and they don't even know how great an impact they had on my life.

P.S. I went to my first DMB concert at the age of 60. I was dancing, singing and holding my own with the young fans. It was exhilarating and just the first of many more to come.

DAVE MATTHEWS BAND

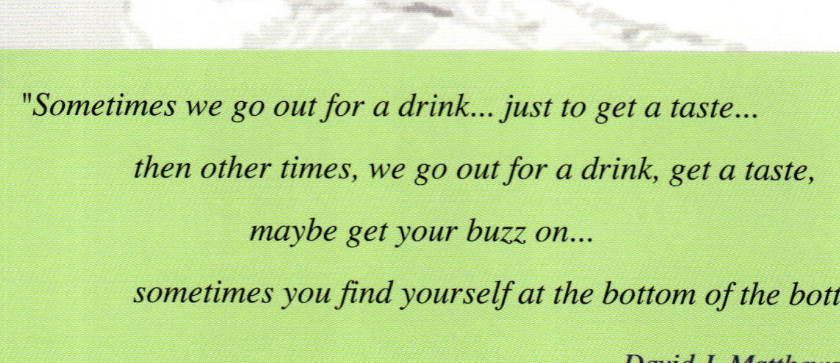

One
drink
to
remember
then
another
to forget
grace

My name is Amy...

I first found the Dave Matthews Band on 'Saturday Night Live" in the early nineties. I bought "Under the Table and Dreaming" the very next day. I had never heard music that moved me so much in my life. I played that CD over and over, It was as if Dave knew my life. His lyrics spoke to me in a very profound way. I could give you my life story and show you how every song is relevant to me, my childhood, my loves, my bipolar disorder, my sex life, my outlook on life and the world. Musically, rhythm and lyrics are what I love ...and no other band can use rhythm combined with such meaningful, insightful, uplifting and sexy lyrics. Before Dave Matthews I listened to alot of music, I am a singer and music has been a part of my life from the beginning. I come from a musical family & spent years on the road singing in bands. In my mind the greatest music had already been made. DMB changed all that! My life has not been easy, I had a rough childhood, I married young and had my first child by the time I was twenty. I was divorced, then married again to a man who abused both me and my first child. Married again and spent years on drugs...had two more children and was diagnosed with bipolar disorder. I survived the 12 years of self-loathing that comes with drug abuse. I turned my life around with the help of modern medicine and a very strong spirit. DMB has been the soundtrack to my life. I have been lifted up over and over by the music. Never has any musician moved me in this way. My life is awesome now...a beautiful life...filled with love, and personal growth. It changes everyday. I see beauty in most everything and Dave just adds the music to fill any silence...to accompany me being me. During the hard times and the good times and the sweet times and the decadent times. Always I love the music. Always.

I almost feel like God speaks to me through Dave, and that is just fine with me.
God Bless Dave.

"Grace is Gone" Trading Card
Series One

Jenn Maroney
D Realm Designs

5 american baby

"Stay beautiful baby
I hope you stay American baby"

11.06

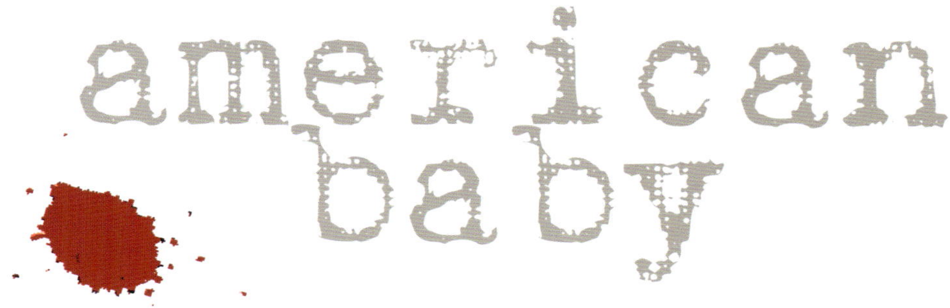

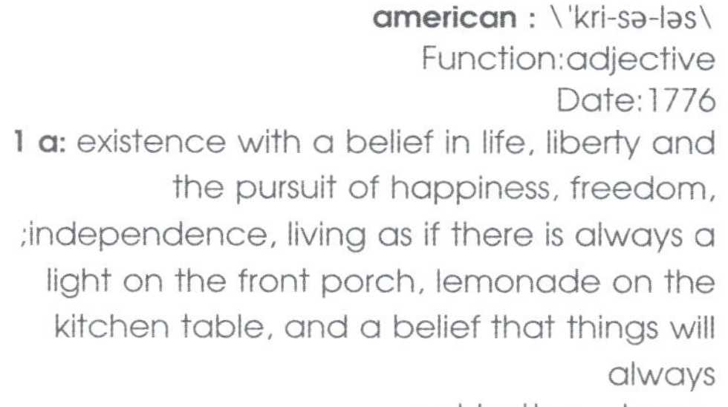

american : \ˈkri-sə-ləs\
Function:adjective
Date:1776
1 a: existence with a belief in life, liberty and the pursuit of happiness, freedom, ;independence, living as if there is always a light on the front porch, lemonade on the kitchen table, and a belief that things will always
get better... hope.

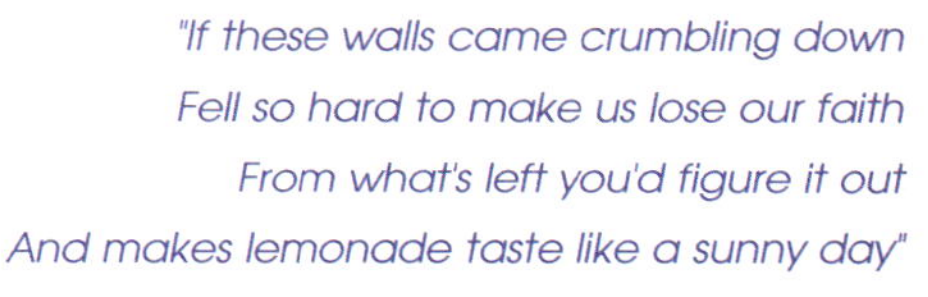

"If these walls came crumbling down
Fell so hard to make us lose our faith
From what's left you'd figure it out
And makes lemonade taste like a sunny day"

Derek

You
lift
me
up
and
always
will.

Have a listen to Derek's beautiful version of "All Along the Watchtower!
http://myspacetv.com/index.cfm?fuseaction=vids.individual&videoid=4782448

All my buddies would be listening to Metallica and stuff before we would go out on missions and raids and I would have my headphones on listening to Dave and Bob Dylan and Leon Russell.

Derek Goff
Broken Arrow, Oklahoma

Brad

"Celebrate we will, 'cause life is short but sweet for certain." A simple quote but yet so, so hard to live by. Dave Matthews Band is full of these quotes that make you think. Only true fans notice or even understand. They have different meanings for everyone who listens and different meanings at different times in our lives. The same words can touch so many people on different levels and for different reasons. This "deep thought", fun, jamming, take-you-away, inspiring, spiritual music has taken me down many roads, holding my hand. They have helped me through the hard times, and helped me make the good times even better.

I started to listen to Dave Matthews Band back in the 90's. I first heard them on the CD player of my "hip" uncle's car after a dinner out with the family. I heard the words, "I eat too much, I drink too much". I flipped out at the beats and the unique freshness of what I was hearing. I was hooked from that day forward and have been a fan ever since.

My life has been riddled with obstacles and hard times. Stories of pain and deep hidden resentment in my life - I will not bore you with those. Depression and the booze are not very good friends of mine indeed. These are the things that anyone may run into during their fast sprint through this thing called "life".

The war in Iraq is one of those many roads I have traveled while Dave and the band held my hand. I was sent over to the sand pit in March of 2003 at the beginning of the war. At that time we thought Saddam had chemical warheads on those missiles he was shooting as we got off that plane. Thoughts of death and pain ran through my head as we departed that plane in Kuwait. There is nothing like having death put right in your face like that from the very beginning. Not a good start I would have to say. That would be instilled with me on throughout my tour. But, when you have to stare at Mr. Death himself, you can't just look away.

When you have to stare at Mr. Death himself, you can't just look away.

One thought brought me away from it all and gave me hope and courage. Yes, my comrades on a daily basis were my first strength. The little moments of downtime - writing letters, playing cards or eating a hot meal were a small refuge, but so was this band called the Dave Matthews Band. That shelter was one of the greatest of all.

f you can imagine that time: a soldier in a large tent waiting with the rest of the guys, on a cot in the middle of the 130 degree day, to get that command to move forward to the center of Iraq. Writing a letter trying to hold the tears back, telling friends and family how much he loved them and that he would be ok- all the time listening with his headphones to the songs, "Everyday" and "Bartender". I was that guy. The times I spent alone with the band were mainly at night. Not every night, but every night I got that chance to drift away to wherever I wanted to drift. I'm not going to list all the songs that meant the most to me during those nights but I think you can imagine the ones that kept me company.

The songs that Dave Matthews has written are full of twists of words and beats that make you get chill bumps in the hot desert. Telling me everything is going to be ok and to enjoy what's all around me because tomorrow we'll be gone. I am a man that tends to forget that by the end of the day in a time of war. But, with some fresh batteries and a little time alone I could get to that happy place and get a recharge.

Whatever your place in life, if at war in a foreign country, problems at home, a party at Joe's house, washing the car on a hot summer day, Dave Matthews Band has a place right there beside you. Dave Matthews Band is just a band, yes, but most bands cannot do what they do. Through all the current so called, "hit's of today", I think one band stands out of that crowd. Whatever the band means to you, I hope that you truly grasp even half of what they mean to me. My past, present and future they will be holding my hand.

Photo by David Adam Beloff

Brad Grier
Florence, Alabama

Eli Hartnett
U.S. Coast Guard

...makes
lemonade
taste like
a sunny day

Band Photos by: David Adam Beloff

Truman

Katrina Meets Dave

When the concerts at Red Rocks were announced in 2005, a good friend of mine from college (Adam Dwinells) and I decided that we couldn't miss the chance to see the boys at such a great and famous amphitheatre. I knew Red Rocks would be gorgeous... mountains, monoliths, the city of Denver behind the stage

I booked some airline tickets and began the search for what would prove to be some of the toughest tickets of the tour. DMB was scheduled to play a 3-night stand in Colorado and with a little luck, I was able to find some pretty good seats for all 3 shows...accumulating more than a few extra pairs in the process. We were getting excited as the date approached and counted the days down about a month away from the concert.

And then Mother Nature provided a change in plans. On August 29, 2005, Hurricane Katrina ripped through the Gulf Coast region. Wreaking havoc on the area, displacing families, flooding entire communities and killing people along the way. The excitement around the concert seemed to fade a little bit as pictures of the destruction and chaos came pouring across the TV screens.

About a day or two later I came up with an idea to get rid of the extra tickets I had. With high demand for this set of shows and the huge amount of people that were still searching for tickets on the warehouse message board I figured that we could put the tickets to good use. It was about 2 weeks before the first concert when I put up a post on the different DMB message boards. It read "Red Cross Charity Ticket Raffle. For $25 your name will be entered into a drawing for one of the 4 pairs of tickets for Red Rocks..." I waited to see if there would be any response to the message. There was. About 600 people had read the posting and a small buzz was started around the idea. I thought about taking the idea in another direction, and mentioned that I was thinking about selling red cups in the parking lots (red cups for the Red Cross and definitely a necessity for your beer.) And this is where the tailgate concept came to life.

I received an e-mail from Rick Grobart. He mentioned that he had seen the posts about the ticket auction and the sale of the beer filled red cups for the Red Cross. He explained to me that he had been working with a group of other Dave Matthews fans that would hold fundraising tailgates in the parking lots before the concerts. The organization was named " Tailgates for a Cause" (www.tailgateforacause.com) and they had already held successful events. Rick explained that we could put together an area where we would give away free food (hot dogs, chips, candy and soft drinks) and simply request donations that would be given to the Red Cross. Beside the food, we would put together a CD of "rare" songs from the summer tour and the previous Dave and Friends Tour. The CDs were given away with a suggested donation of $20... we weren't ever selling anything and made the music available in a downloadable format for those that did not care to donate.

Well this sounded like a great idea to me and became a full time project for the next 2 weeks. I threw up another post on different places on the Internet and asked if anyone would be interested in trying to pull off this event. The response was pretty amazing. People from all over the country, even people that would not physically be at the concerts wrote e-mails with their offers to help.

Andi Cannata was one of those people. She had worked with Rick on previous TFAC events and was an avid fundraiser/ all around good person. She pledged to provide all of the burnt CDs that we would need through our event, more than 500 in total. She utilized the network of people that had e-mailed their offers to help and told me to take it off the list of things to be done.

As the event came together, it became obvious that there was a lot of work to be done and a good number of people would be required to pull this off. Not once did we have a shortage of people.
"100 times...1000 times."
Fans from all across the country pitched in to make each day perfect.
Ben walks over and says, "Need a little help?"
Casey says, "Got you covered."
And finally, " Anyone got a ticket?"
Yes, give it to Glen Walker.

Oh, yeah...I got one final message. "Can I match whatever you raise?"
Not a bad e-mail.

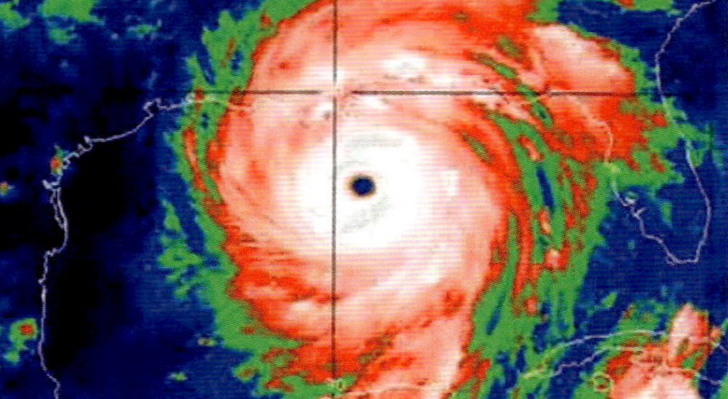

"We can do something good. It's good when we all get together. We can make something good."

- David J. Matthews

9.11.05 Red Rocks - Morrison, CO

SPENCE
Thank you for your courage.

Chief Petty Officer Spencer Dyson
U.S. Navy

During our first two years of marriage, Spence deployed frequently while serving aboard a submarine. While he was gone, he'd write in journals for me. Since he was gone more than half the time, this was the way we stayed close. During "underways" when he couldn't listen to music, he would write out lyrics to Dave's songs in the journals for comfort. "Bartender" was a particular favorite of his, so it was especially poignant for us when Dave dedicated a performance of that song to those serving in the military on 3/20/07 (Live Trax Volume 8). We also have "I'll Back You Up" engraved in our wedding bands and feel it is a very appropriate song for couples dealing with the challenges of military life. When I was lucky enough to meet Dave in 2005, I told him all about Spence (who unfortunately wasn't with me). Dave not only signed an autograph for him, but wrote him a note: "Spence-Thank you for your courage."

The USS MONTEREY (CG-61) homecoming. After 6 months out to sea, the Captain gave our band, "Gear Adrift" permission to play outside on the decks where everyone could hear us... (we had some really powerfull speakers...hehe).

Here we were actually playing "So Much to Say"!

Morgan Terry
U.S. Navy

Stay beautiful baby.

"Gear Adrift"

crush 6

"It's crazy, I'm thinking,
just knowing that the world is round,
And here I'm dancing on the ground,
Am I right=side-up or upside-down,
And is this real or am I dreaming?"

09.06

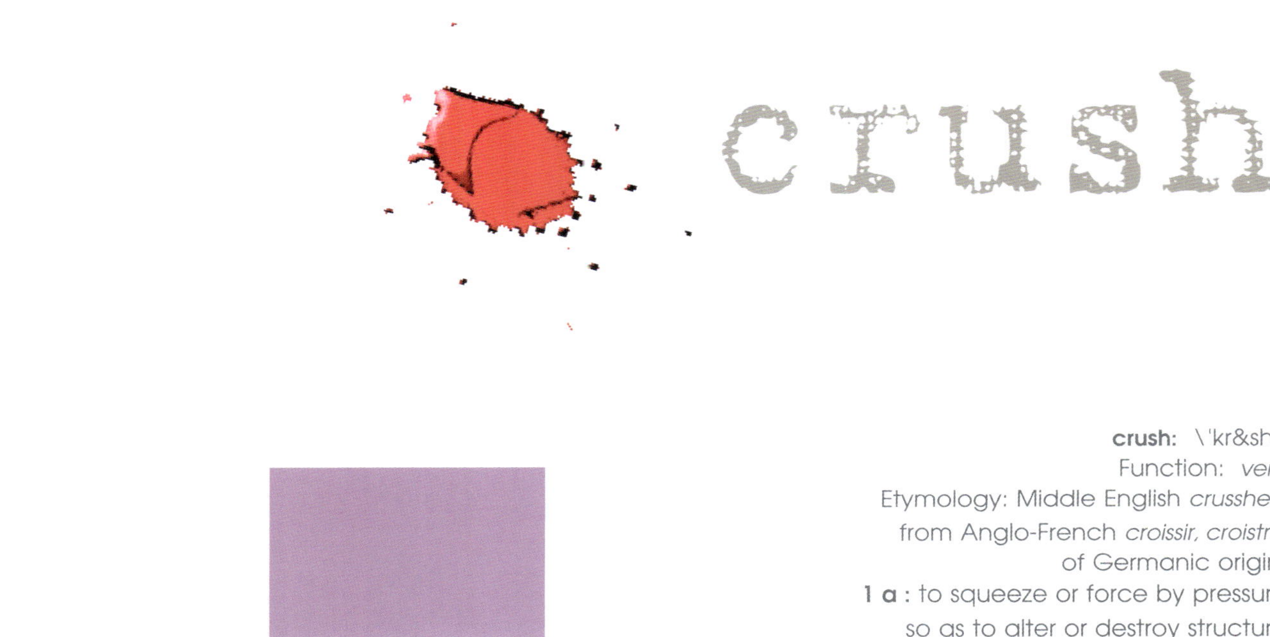

crush: \'kr&sh\
Function: *verb*
Etymology: Middle English *crusshen,* from Anglo-French *croissir, croistre,* of Germanic origin.
1 a : to squeeze or force by pressure so as to alter or destroy structure <*crush* grapes> **2 :** HUG, EMBRACE **3 a :** to suppress or overwhelm as if by pressure or weight **b :** to subdue completely

"Crazy, how it feels tonight
Crazy, how you make it all alright, love
Crush me with the things you do
And I'll do for you, anything, too, oh
Sitting, smoking, feeling high,
And in this moment, oh, it feels so right"

Randall's Island 2006

Since I was old enough to know the difference between boys and girls, Jared has been my boy in life. Our moms worked together, our dads worked together, my Mee-Maw was his teacher in grade school--we were always together. As shy as he was growing up, he eventually opened up
to me and by the time middle school rolled around and we were finally at the same school, Jared was one of my first "boyfriends" but he ended up breaking up with me for a different Ashley, who had long blonde hair and I didn't. I spent most of middle and high school trying to stay as close to Jared as I could. Every other guy that I wanted to ask me on a date or to go to a dance did, but I could never catch Jared's eye, so I gave up. I had convinced myself that I was only Ashley the best friend and I would never be anything else. He politely reminded me of this by taking blonde Ashley to prom senior year. High school and graduation came and went and everyone went their separate ways. I went to college and the first week of college had found the guy I thought I was going to spend the rest of my life with. Wrong! It was an abusive relationship. Jared was out of my life for two years. I was looking forward to spending the summer at home reconnecting with my family and seeing friends I had known since pre-school. The first time I saw everyone again, no one asked questions, it was almost as if they knew what I had been through, although, I never told anyone. Jared saw me and gave me a hug and said, "Hey, loser, where have you been? Good to see you." I've never been so glad to see him. It was that night they invited me to join the gang for all their Dave trips that summer and I happily accepted. It was the first thing I had looked forward to in a long time.

June 12th and 13th 2005, DMB was in Noblesville, Ind. and those are shows we always go to because it's only a couple hours north of our hometown. On the second night, it was only me and three of my guy friends, one of them being Jared. One of the guys gets a little friendly when he's drinking, so when

Someone grabbed me from behind and started dancing with me

I assumed it was him. But when I turned my head slighty, I saw it was Jared. He didn't say anything, I didn't say anything. We just swayed with the music and every second that went by, he held me tighter. Neither of us said anything about that night. None of our other friends knew that moment had happened and I told myself he was just being nice, that he was lonely or he had been drinking, although, I knew he hadn't had a drop all night.

Ashley
Indiana

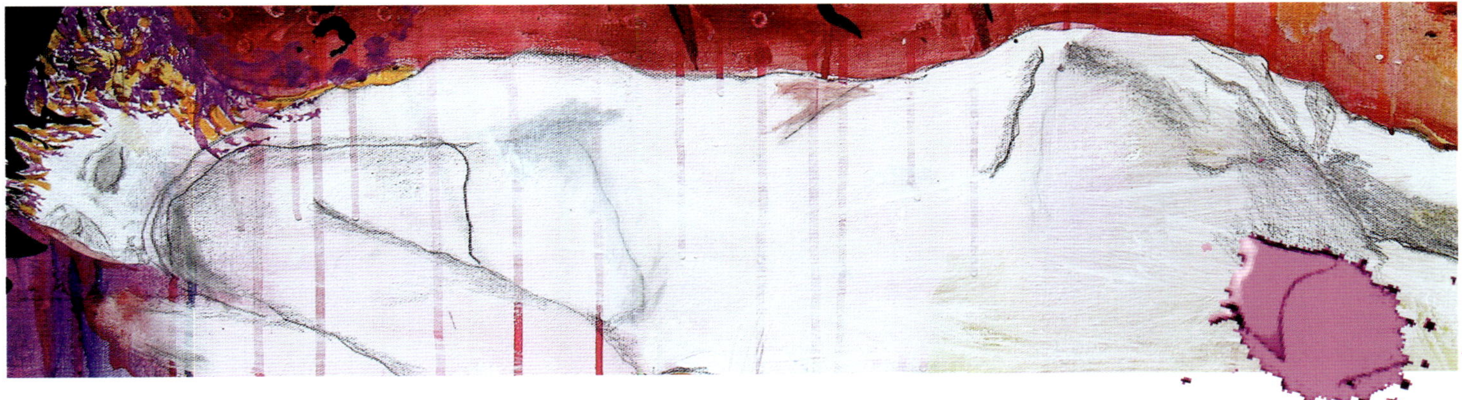

July 20th, 2005, DMB was in Nashville, TN and a group of us loaded up again and headed south. During the concert, DMB played " Crush". I knew it was Jared's favorite, but I had always known that and was surprised that he didn't show his enthusiasm that he was finally hearing it live. Instead, he put his arms around me and sang to me.

" It's crazy, I'm thinking, just as long as you're around,
And here I'll be dancing on the ground
Am I right-side-up or upside-down?
To each other we'll be facing, my love, my love
We'll beat back the pain we've found
You know, I mean to tell you all the things
I've been thinking deep inside
My friend,
Each moment, the more I love you
Crush me.
C'mon baby."

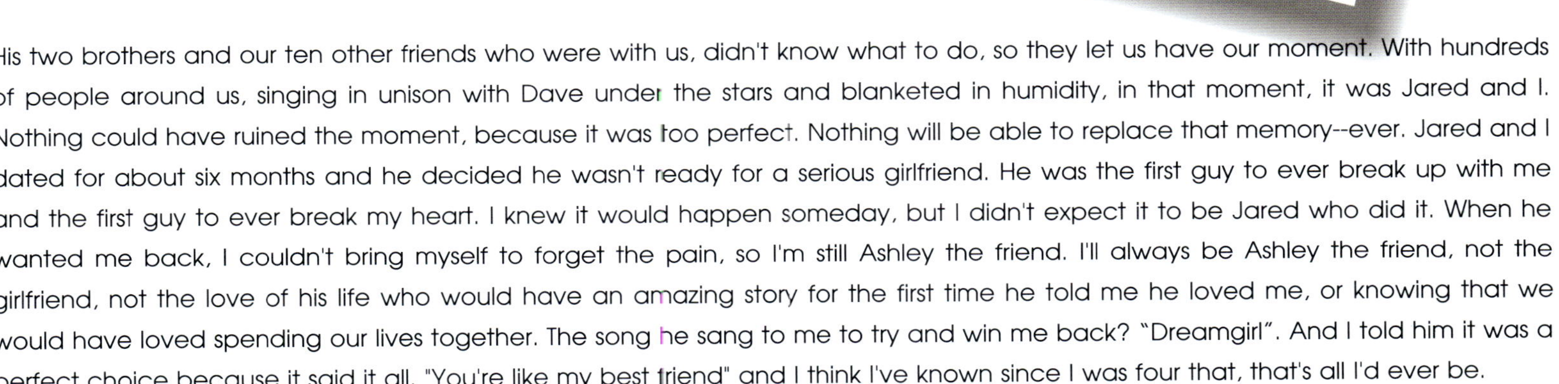

His two brothers and our ten other friends who were with us, didn't know what to do, so they let us have our moment. With hundreds of people around us, singing in unison with Dave under the stars and blanketed in humidity, in that moment, it was Jared and I. Nothing could have ruined the moment, because it was too perfect. Nothing will be able to replace that memory--ever. Jared and I dated for about six months and he decided he wasn't ready for a serious girlfriend. He was the first guy to ever break up with me and the first guy to ever break my heart. I knew it would happen someday, but I didn't expect it to be Jared who did it. When he wanted me back, I couldn't bring myself to forget the pain, so I'm still Ashley the friend. I'll always be Ashley the friend, not the girlfriend, not the love of his life who would have an amazing story for the first time he told me he loved me, or knowing that we would have loved spending our lives together. The song he sang to me to try and win me back? "Dreamgirl". And I told him it was a perfect choice because it said it all. "You're like my best friend" and I think I've known since I was four that, that's all I'd ever be.

It was as if this night was the only night that ever was.

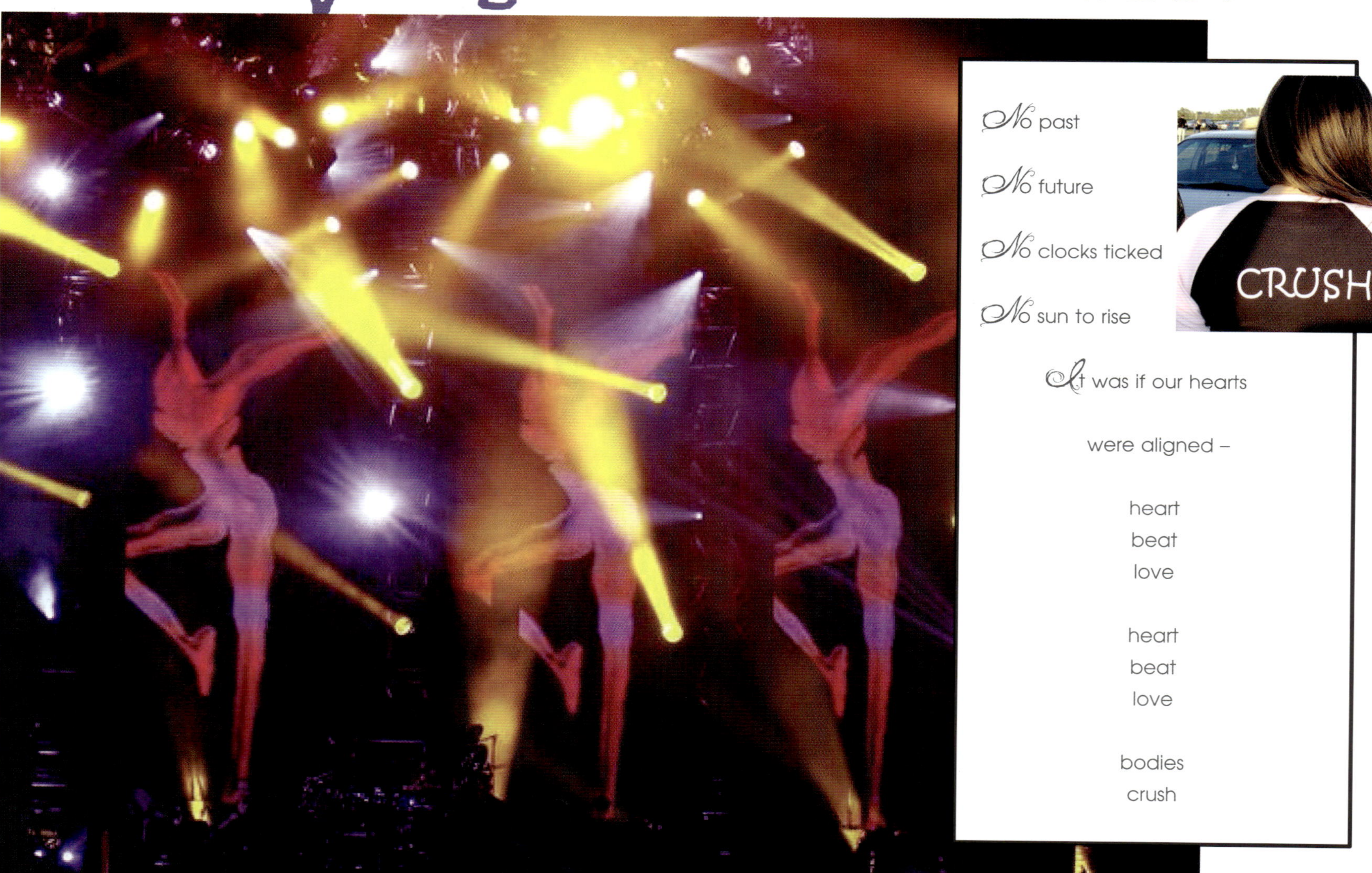

No past

No future

No clocks ticked

No sun to rise

It was if our hearts

were aligned –

heart
beat
love

heart
beat
love

bodies
crush

Camden, NJ 2007

Chantel

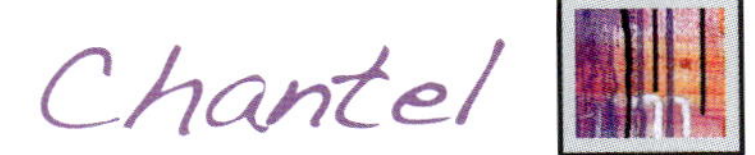

Our relationship had been passionate but sticky since the first day we laid eyes on each other. There was an intense feeling that everyone could feel when we were together. Electric! After barely getting to start, I was afraid things were over between my "friend" and me...That was until August 8, 2004--DMB @ Alpine Valley. I had never been to a Dave show before, but he knew what we were both in for. He knew we were going to dance together in the setting sun. He knew we would be one with the moment and the music. He knew we would experience something significant together. This was our last chance to connect before we both left for seperate colleges. This one night was one that would make or break us forever. Waiting in the never ending line of cars outside of Alpine Valley was enough to make anyone a fan forever. The ambiance of the venue touches your senses and your soul. Nothing beats 40,000+ people in one beautiful place for one beautiful event. There is an energy which cannot be described, only felt by us. I am lucky enough to look back at that night and know that this is the place and the time where he and I became "us". I will mark my anniversary each and every year with that memory. Dave concerts at Alpine have become a ritual, even now living in Tennessee. I will forever be able to think back and feel the songs that were played and the way we danced under those stars. I will forever be able to remember the night I fell in love...

"Crush" playing in the background at my first Dave Matthews Band show.

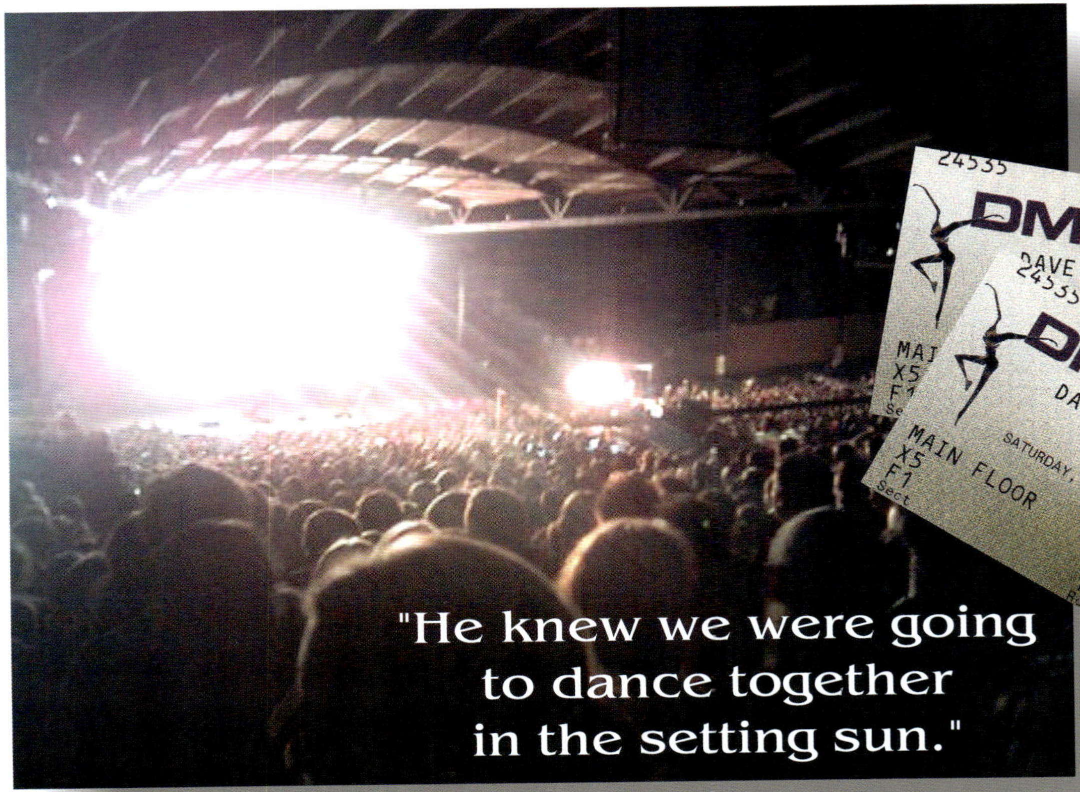
"He knew we were going
to dance together
in the setting sun."

Chantel
Milwaukee, WI

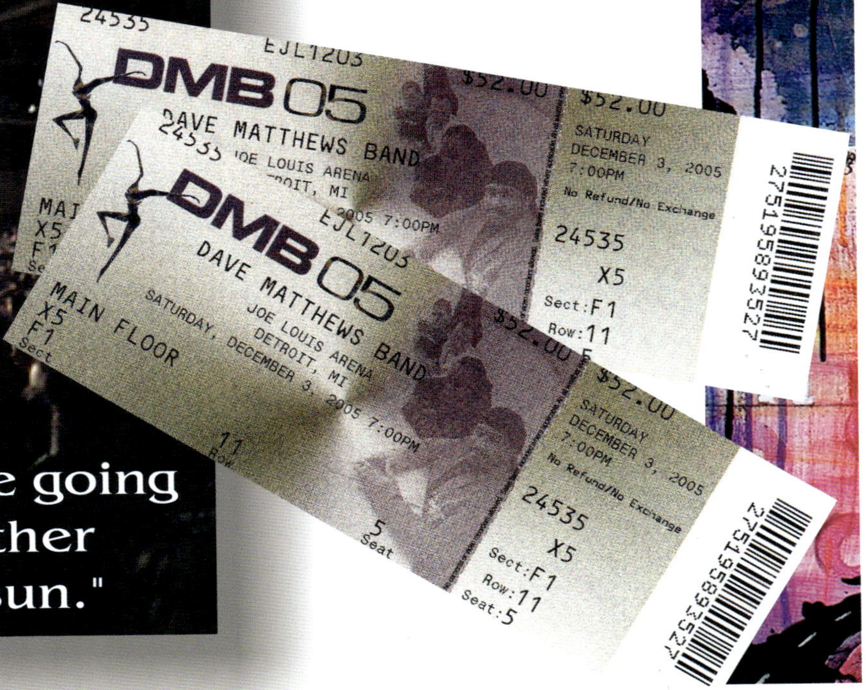
DMB 05
DAVE MATTHEWS BAND
JOE LOUIS ARENA
DETROIT, MI
SATURDAY, DECEMBER 3, 2005 7:00PM
MAIN FLOOR
$52.00
SATURDAY
DECEMBER 3, 2005
7:00PM
No Refund/No Exchange
24535
X5
Sect:F1
Row:11
Seat:5
2751958935527

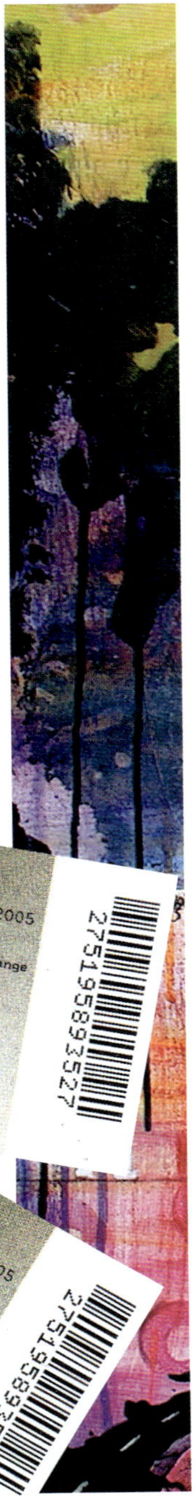

"Crush" Sketch

"Crush" Artist Trading Card
Series 4

"So when your starin' up at the sky and dreamin', 'cause when your dreamin' that's the only real free place, is in your head, everywhere else there's someone else tellin' you what to do then you stare up at the stars and maybe once in awhile some of them move."

-- David J. Matthews

07.31.95 - Austin , TX

PHOTO BY: WWW.DAVIDADAM.NET

Let's go drive til morning comes
Watch the sun rise to fill up our souls
under this spell

CRUSH #2
02. 07

7
i'll back you up

"And for sure we have danced
In the risk of each other
Would like to dance
Around the world with me?"

02. 07

i'll back you up

risk : \'risk\
Function: *noun*
Etymology: French *risque,* from Italian *risco*
1 : possibility of loss or injury : **PERIL**
2 : someone or something that creates or suggests a hazard

"And for sure we have danced
In the risk of each other
Would like to dance
Around the world with me?"

Morgan

"Will you marry me?"

Morgan purchased the painting inspired by "I'll Back You Up" as a gift for Ashley. How perfect that when he planned his "I-am-going-to-ask-Ashley-to-marry-me" treasure hunt complete with a treasure map, that on the final stop of the hunt, he presented this book to her and asked her to have a look . . . you might imagine how shocked she was to come upon this surprise page!

And, of course, she said "yes"!!

Chelley

Kevin and I couldn't be more different!! He's metal and I am all "hippie-like" (as he puts it! Hee hee)! He's all Pantera and Black Sabbath and Ozzy. I'm all peace and love and Hendrix and save-the-planet! When we first got together, we had nothing in common! Then we began to get to know each other. A month cr two into our gig, we both found out that we had this love for DMB. It was always there for me but he knew a few tunes, too. He never told anyone, but grew to like them more and more as we grew together. He would tell me that "Crush" reminded him of me. I called him my "Rapunzel" coz of his long hair! 8 loooong and fun years later, we still share that same passion! Every summer is exciting coz we both enjoy seeing the band and all the wonderful FRIENDS we have met over the years!! It's amazing how something as simple as tunes can bring people together.

chelley & kevin

Over the years it's always been "OHHHH! That's our song". Sometimes we think they were written just for us! It was on our wedding day that it really hit me! On the way to meet him, I popped in a cd. Now picture me…my makeup perfect. I looked beautiful! Then the songs came…"I'll Back You Up", "Lover Lay Down", "Crush". I had no idea "our songs" were on that cd...I lost it. My makeup smeared. My mascara ran down my cheeks but I was sooo happy and couldn't wait to marry him.

This picture is of the three of us that day...

Kevin, me and my firedancer!

" Walk where you like, your steps.
Do as you please, I'll back you up"

kristen & casey

oscar & days

steve & ceason

mike & misty

"I have a message from Bill who is in the 7th row. This message is a request. It says DAVE - PLEASE play "Lover Lay Down" because if you play that, I will get laid by my girlfriend, Jill." (Then Dave says,) "Hey Bill, I wrote the damn song, if anything, Jill and I should be getting it on tonight!"

- David J. Matthews

01.20.07 Hass Auditorium (Bloomsburg University) - Bloomsburg, PA

justin & jennifer

We were married in Vegas

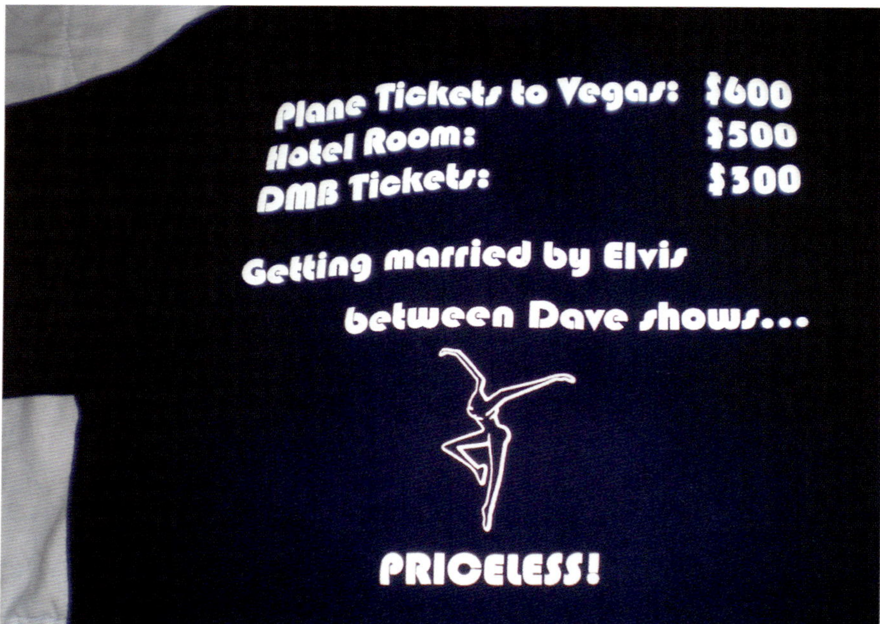

...between the Dave shows!

We were married in March 2007 in Vegas....yes between the Dave shows on Saturday March 24th. We planned our wedding around the Vegas shows and had 30 friends and family make the trip with us. For our wedding party which were mostly our closest friends and our parents we gave them all tickets to the Saturday nite show. We all got to sit together, it was pretty awesome. I have never felt as much love between my friends and family as I did at that show. Jeremy's brother and his wife made up tee shirts for for the wedding party.

We all wore them to the show that nite!

We were quite a sight walking through the MGM.

We looked like a school field trip!

krystal & ben

As a fan, I am happy to say that when my husband and I were first getting to know each other, our first official date was a DMB concert.

My second son's name is David Matthew.

After many years of contemplation, this year I finally got a tattoo to celebrate the two loves of my life (besides my family):
the sun and Dave Matthews Band.

Renae 

My boyfriend and I have been together for five years now. We started dating when I was 16, he was 17 and we've known each other since we were 12 and 13 years old. After dating for two years, we moved out together into our first apartment. Things were so wonderful and then we had moved out of the apartment into a house that a family friend owned. To make a long story short, living in that house had really affected our relationship. We were fighting all the time and getting to the point where we both thought it was over. He left for a few weeks and we ended up reconciling and decided to try to make it work. Throughout our entire relationship, we're always gone to all of DMB's shows at the Gorge every year and we've been HUGE fans for about 10 years now. Well, one night we were driving to my parent's house, and at this point, we had gotten back together but still were losing hope and didn't have too much faith left in us and our relationship. As we were driving I put in "Everday" and "Space Between" came on. I had always loved this song but that night, I really thought about our relationship while listening to it. I started crying. Justin, my boyfriend, pulled over and asked what was wrong. I told him to just listen to it and think about our relationship while listening to it. He also started crying after doing this. The lyrics in that song gave us hope. When Dave says, "Take my hand ' cuz we're walking out of here", it hit us. We needed to put our relationship first, before anything, in order to save it. We needed to take each other's hand and walk out of that place our relationship was in.

"Look at us spinning out in the madness of a rollercoaster
You know you went off like the devil in the church
In the middle of a crowded room
All we can do my love
Is hope we don't take this ship down"

Basically I was the "devil going off" and all we really could do was hope we didn't ruin our relationship.

Now my boyfriend, Justin, and I are engaged and will be getting married within the next year (no date set yet). We now are stronger than ever and are able to keep our faith whenever anything happens because we know we got through how bad it really was with us. When we look back on it, we know now we were younger, still learning how to be in a committed relationship and still have our own separate lives. If we hadn't really listened to that song, and have that light bulb go off in our heads, we might not be together today. He is my rock, and I am his. We are everything to each other and now songs like "Steady as We Go" and "Crash" are our "motto" songs. He and I have a crazy connection that no matter what we do, it doesn't go away and our love never fades. Without Dave and his music, we might not have been able to realize any of that.

Renae
Auburn, WA

Somehow
we keep up
with
each other.

Randall's Island 2005

Song for a song

(I'll back you up)

So here we are, the greatest few we are,
Lost in a world of sounds that fills my soul
And your soul with the emptiness of a miracle.
Tonight's the night of the 1000 fires
That burn wild in our lips
With the explosion of silence.
Dance, dance, dance
Dance over me
Like the bird in the bible,
Dance around me
Like if I were a bonfire
And you a barefooted foot.
Give me a break,
Just a minute on the sand of night:
I'm up again to dance
Around the world with you.

dreamgirl 8

"I would dig a hole all the way to China
Unless of course I was there
Then I'd dig my way home."

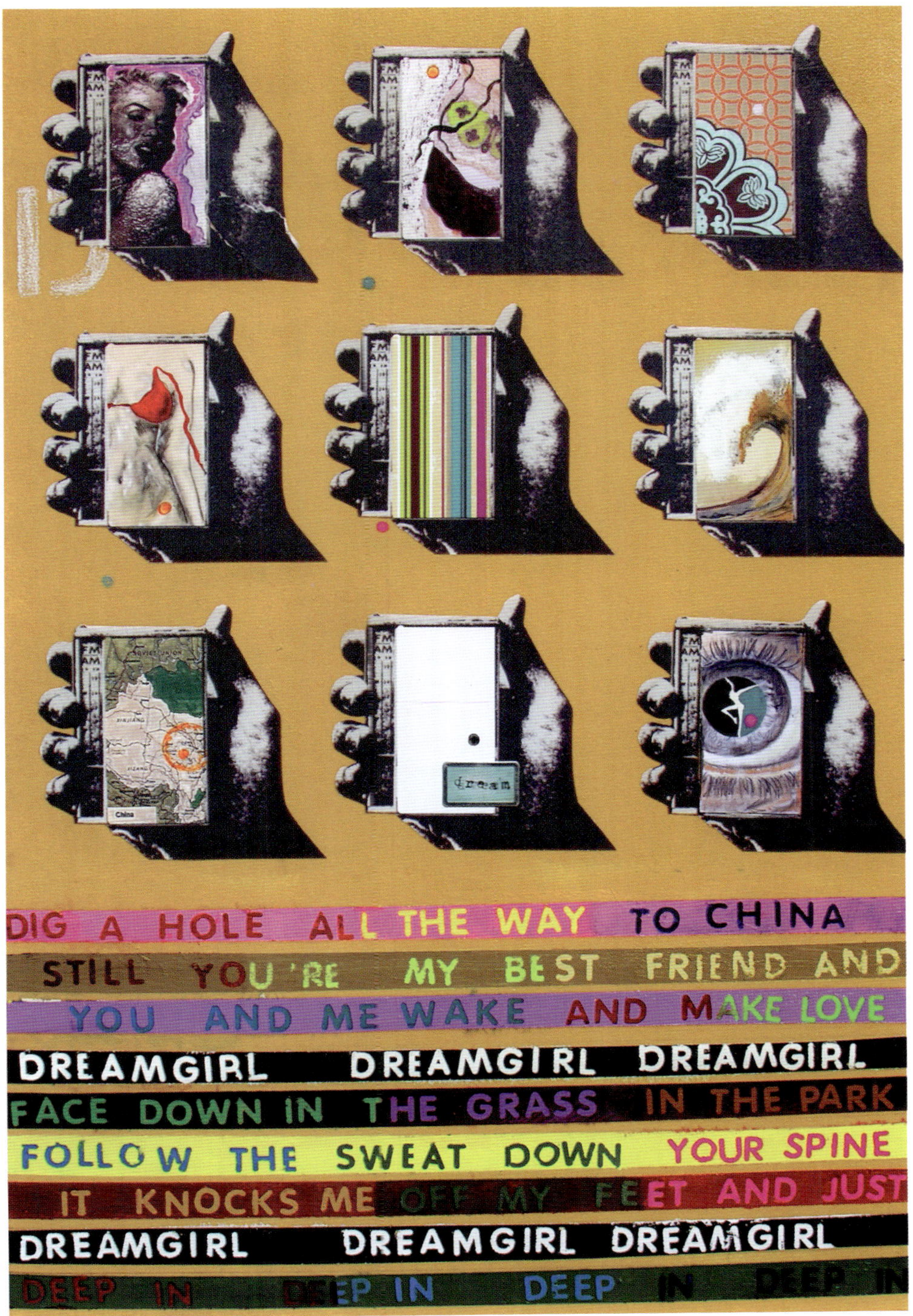
DIG A HOLE ALL THE WAY TO CHINA
STILL YOU'RE MY BEST FRIEND AND
YOU AND ME WAKE AND MAKE LOVE
DREAMGIRL DREAMGIRL DREAMGIRL
FACE DOWN IN THE GRASS IN THE PARK
FOLLOW THE SWEAT DOWN YOUR SPINE
IT KNOCKS ME OFF MY FEET AND JUST
DREAMGIRL DREAMGIRL DREAMGIRL
DEEP IN DEEP IN DEEP IN DEEP IN
China
dream

08.07

dreamgirl: \'drEm 'g&r(-&)l\
Function: *noun*
Usage: *often attributive*
Etymology: Middle English *dreem,* from Old English *drEam* noise, joy, and Old Norse *draumr* dream;
1a: a girl notable for her beauty, excellence, or enjoyable quality <I was dreaming of a dreamgirl>
4 a : a strongly desired woman b : something that fully satisfies a wish : IDEAL

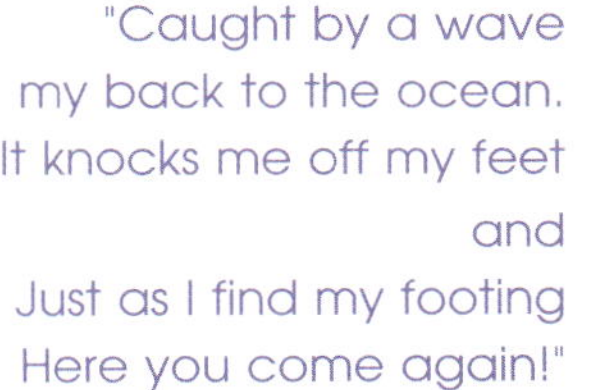

"Caught by a wave
my back to the ocean.
It knocks me off my feet
and
Just as I find my footing
Here you come again!"

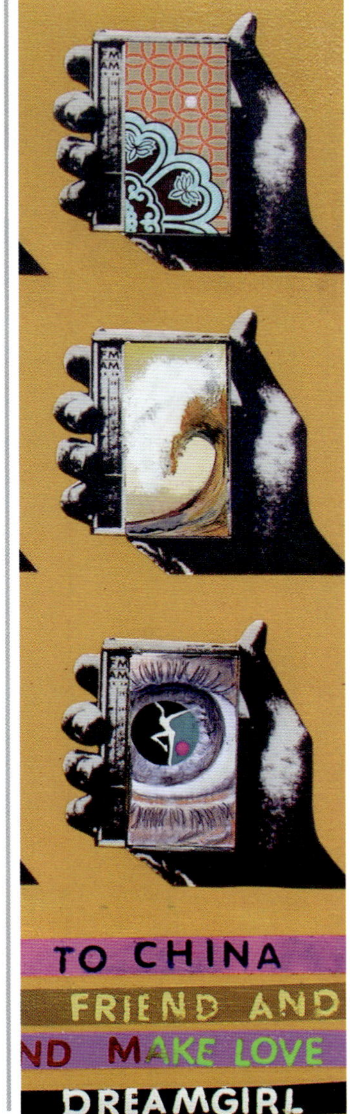

I was dreamin' of a dreamgirl . . .

Rob

I smiled. I mean I really smiled. It was Christmas, my birthday and the day that Sara G. made all my dreams come true in 10th grade all wrapped up in one! I had been waiting almost 2 years. Last year my brother got married so there was the wedding and my Grandfather died so there was the funeral. Business in Tampa while the band was in Camden and Bud (my bulldog) had a kidney infection while the band was at Fenway! So this was the day I had waited for ...Dave Matthews Band was in town and there was nothing but open road between me and Saratoga! No issues...no drama...no dog problems...In less than 8 hours, I would be underneath a starlit sky listening to Dave and Carter and Leroi and Boyd and Stefan and Raswawn and Butch make my heart fly!! Ah ...no feeling like it.

Cooler packed. Guiness on ice. Grill semi-clean. A sausage. Some burgers. My friends Dan and John. Good to go! 45 minutes to the parking lot. 45 more minutes to park. Crowded as usual. Nothing had changed. The air full of expectation.

We found a good place to park under a grove of small trees. It had to have been 90 degrees in the shade that day. Dan got the grill ready while I set up a couple of chairs and got my guitar out. The day was perfect...some tunes...some beer...friends...food from the grill! It was heaven.

"I usually am not the smoothest operator."

Then I saw her...she lay on a blanket in the middle of an open area. On her stomach in the midst of dandelions. Longish brown hair. Orange tank top. Jeans. She looked as though she was asleep. I knew right there and then that I needed to know her. I am usually not the smoothest operator but like I said, I HAD to know her so I grabbed my guitar, walked over to her blanket, grabbed a corner and in my very best Dave imitation, began singing.

"Caught by a wave my back to the ocean. It knocks me off my feet and just as I find my footing, here you come again!..." A little corny, I know...

She raised her head slowly, her eyes blinking like she had just woken up. She looked into my eyes. She brushed a piece of hair away from her face. She wiped a drip of sweat from her cheek. Then as I finished the last chorus, she did the wildest thing – she sat up and reached across the quilt to take my face between her hands. She kissed me. We knew that something was beginning for us. We spent the next 3 hours on that blanket. I sang. She smiled. I forgot about the grill and even the beer!

The sausage

We managed to talk our friends into switching seats and spent the entire evening together just jamming to Dave and lost in the rhythm of the band and each other. There was nothing but this night and her hips dancing and Dave singing and a spirit that lifted me higher and higher. But too soon, the show was over. Before she left with her friends, she handed me her ticket stub. On it was her cell number.

I knew this was what I had been waiting for. Her face. Her smile. Her spirit. Everything I had dreamed of! And she loved the band!

Just as my friends and I pulled out of the parking lot, the rain began. Huge drops falling. I wished I were home now so I could go back and relive the day. I grabbed the back seat and let John drive. The sun and the beer and the beauty of this day had gotten to me and I fell sound asleep. I awoke suddenly to the sound of Dan's "Look out!" Our car was spinning around in circles in the middle of the wet highway. It kept spinning for what seemed forever and then slowly stopped. Not a car in sight. "So Damn Lucky" was blasting from the speakers! We were safe but the trunk had flown open and our stuff lay strewn across the road. We gathered up everything- thankful that the road was empty but wishing we had a flashlight or something. When we arrived home that night, we were all thankful to be alive! I sat down at my kitchen table with my backpack. I just wanted to see her number. To know the day was real. I reached into the small pocket that held the ticket stub and pulled it out. It was soaked and wrinkled. Part of the number was gone. I couldn't read it! Washed away…gone…nothing…

I know she is somewhere out there. Dancing in the sun, breathing in beauty,

Could it have been you?

The ticket

the girl

WAREHOUSE

MY dreamgirl...
My beautiful wife Leah...
she embodies every aspect of the
word "love".

Mansfield, MA
7.05

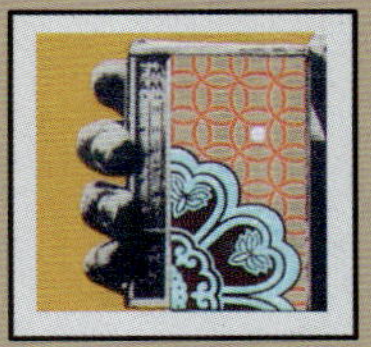

I WOULD DIG A HOLE ALL THE WAY TO CHINA
dave matthews band
with special guest
THE FRAY

"Still you're my best friend."

DMB

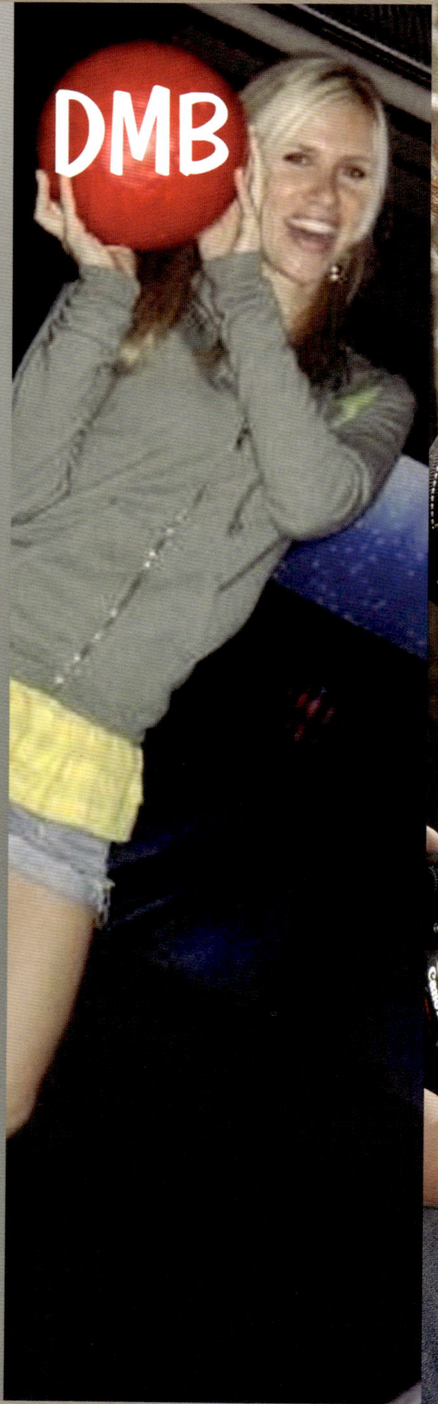

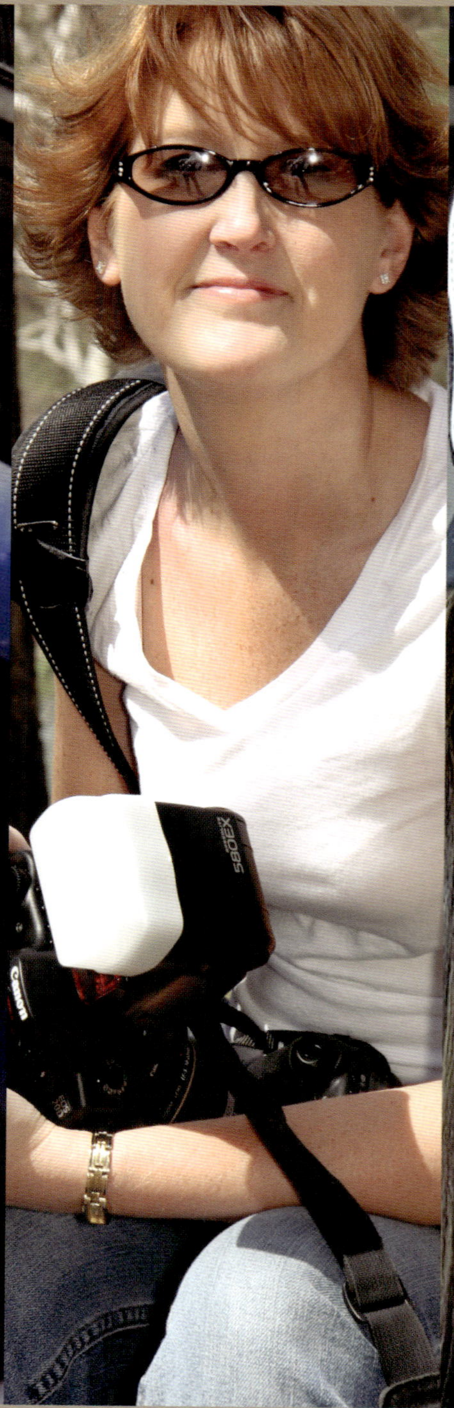

dmb

Terri 

Why did they do this for ME?

For quite some time, probably since 2003, I have been an active member on nancies.org message boards, particularly with a group of mostly women who post daily on a thread affectionately known as "Housewives from Hell". The group is pretty big, but somehow we keep up with each other's families, friends, etc., talking about all sorts of things from our dmb obsession to what's for dinner tonight to dealing with pregnancies, miscarriages, adoptions, child care, love, divorce, addiction problems, etc. The list goes on and on. We really just have fun, laughing, crying, planning our tour dates, discussing setlists, supporting each other, coming up with ideas to help one another, cheering each other on when starting out a new endeavor, and bitching (of course) about whatever is bugging us at the moment. This all began because of one common thread - we all love Dave Matthews Band. We came there to share in that love, and we got something really unexpected - true friendships!!! It's amazing to think that I made friends all over the country (and in Canada!) without having met any of them initially. Yet over time, I endedup hosting many of them in my home for visits or stays while in town for dmb shows, not an uncommon thing in the dmb community, but new to me!!! So now you know a little background, which is a beautiful story itself because the women I've met through that thread have been one of the greatest blessings I've received. The timing couldn't have been better, too, because I was going through some tough times in my life beginning in 2004. The details aren't significant to the story, but I'll just say I really needed support and there was plenty given by these wonderful friends. They were always there with encouraging words, thoughtful input and even questions for me to consider that often helped me know what I needed to do.

Early in 2005, I was emailing with one of these amazing friends who lives in Seattle. We were discussing tickets for upcoming summer shows, etc.. At some point she just casually informs me that I'm going to the Gorge in August. I'm thinking..."no, you silly girl, I'm not going to the Gorge". True that is has been my dream to go, but remember, I live on the east coast and cannot afford to fly round trip plus three nights of tickets and who knows what else for lodging, food, etc. She replies that, yes, in fact, I am going. That everything has been arranged. I will have plane tickets and show tickets, will be camping with a group of our friends, and will have transportation to and from the airport. She adds that she has even exchanged emails with a family member to make sure that child care for my two kids will be covered. I read this, shaking, just unable to truly comprehend what the words mean. To summarize, she rallied up a group of our friends who had the means to help get me to the gorge, and simply put - they made it happen. From donating money, frequent flier miles, their time, their spare room, camping gear...they did it all. For what? Why did they do this for ME? Because they are remarkable friends, because they recognized the very hard times I had been enduring the past year and found a way to give me a gift I can never repay. The true bottom line of this story is they made my dream come true. Honestly, that is what it was. I must say from the time I left for Seattle to the time I arrived back home in Virginia, I had the best time of my life. Seriously. I think it was a combination of where I was in my life at the time, the gift of what these amazing women did for ME, being surrounded by the amazing wonder that IS the Gorge...it was truly magical. I have never had such joy as spending the days with my friends in the Gorge campground, then making the trek to the ampitheatre each night to become one with the music that IS Dave Matthews Band.

a family connected -
united -
not through blood
coarsing through our
veins
but by the collective
energy of the music.
reaching our very
hearts and souls!
-Ceason

"Housewives from Hell"

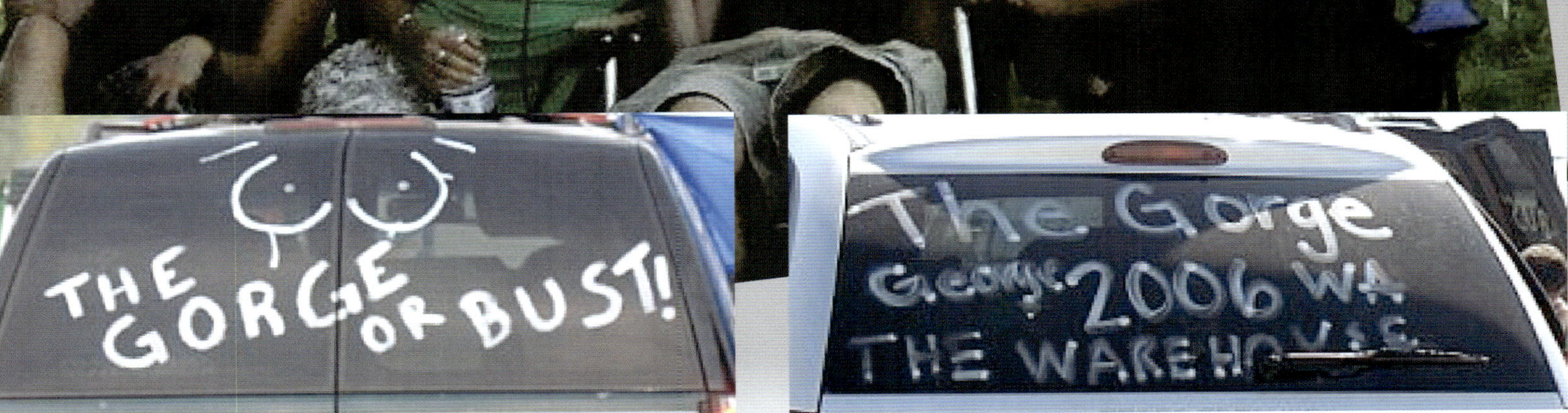

A Special Acoustic Evening With
DAVE MATTHEWS & TIM REYNOLDS
SUNDAY APRIL 22
SOLD OUT
DAVE MATTHEWS BAND
SINCE 1991
DAVE MATTHEWS BAND
20 06

D M B

I was fortunate enough to join the Warehouse the day it opened (12/4/98), thus I've been spoiled for tickets, and have become accustomed to sitting in the first 5-10 rows for shows where seniority is invoked. This also puts me in 'poster distance', that is to say that if I bring a poster, Dave's sure to read it. While, for the last 5 years or so, for all the shows that I've been to that I've sat close enough, I bring a poster that says "Vusi To Open Winter DMB Tour". I only flash it for a second or two, and only when Dave's looking over. But, each time I bring it he ends up pointing at me for a few seconds and making a face (like "way to go", or a thumbs up, or he'll point at his head). I had told Vusi the story about the poster (I've been fortunate enough to meet him as well, and lucky enough to have lunch with him in Chicago a few years ago). Well, last year when Vusi came to Chicago, I actually brought one of the posters from the DMB show a few weeks prior. Vusi got a kick out of it, and when we took pictures, he insisted we take one with the poster.

Right before his wedding, Rick wrote this email to a group of his friends:

So my just-as-fanatical-maybe-more friend "A" mentioned to me over the weekend that Dave will be shooting a video in Chicago on Monday (today), and she'd find out where on Monday morning and if it would be a closed set or open. She calls me Monday and says it's at the Music Box (my favorite movie theater, renovated from the 1930's and shows strictly foreign and independent flicks) and it's a closed set. Explains that because of some logistical headaches, she couldn't make it but gave me her blessing to go ahead.

Uh-oh. I have a 1:00 appointment to check out tuxedoes for our wedding, and a 6:30 flight to Tampa for work. Other than that, I had the day planned to catch up on a little paperwork at my home. Through Jean and my stepmother's good graces, we move the tuxedo appointment to noon. I head to the Music Box after we finish up. Grab an iced chai across the street and nonchalantly walk past the theater which had tons of gear trucks in front of it. Like an ass, I ask what's going on inside. The cop (yeah, cop) says they are shooting a commercial inside. "Oh", and I move on. Not sure what I'm going to say or do, or how to make the most of the moment, I hand around outside in the boiling heat, blue jeans, and a white t-shirt. While I'm contemplating it I see a bunch of helper guys coming in and out in blue jeans and white t-shirt. Apparently I dressed in their uniform…and, not all of 'em had passes on!

After a while (about 30 minutes) I see them pull up a white van in front of the place, indicating to me that the band may be going to make a quick exit. Not wanting to make a street scene, I swing my car around back just in time to see a gear truck pull away, and an open door to the alley. Park my car and mozie into the back door of the Music Box. Yes, there were a lot of people. Yes, my heart was about to jump out of my chest. Yes, Dave Matthews was inside.

There's a huge food spread, and loads of cameras – in the theater and in the main concession area. All the folks are in the concession area, where Dave is finalizing some shots with the director. I try to fade into the background, which isn't too hard to do since I'm (again) accidentally wearing roadie-gear. Rather than look at Dave, I'm looking at the monitors as if I have something important to do and I'm really thinking about it. A few minutes later, the director yells "That's a wrap." Dave thanks all the guys around him (I'm not around him, rather faded about 20' back) and exits into the small theater, where his dressing room is set up. About 5 minutes later he comes out and chats with the director. As he's getting ready to leave I tap his arm. He turns to me and the conversation goes something like this.

"Hi Dave, great shoot today"

"Yeah, everything seemed to flow"

"I have nothing to do with the shoot, and I'm not supposed to be here, but worked my way in. Just wanted to say I've been to tons of shows and have a great time every time. And, I want to know if you're going to have Vusi open any of the shows any times soon".

"You know Vusi?" says Dave.

"Yep, I'm a huge fan of his. I usually bring a sign to the shows that says 'VUSI TO OPEN DMB WINTER DMB TOUR"

"That's you?"

"Yeah, no one ever understands it. In fact, I've been into the South African music scene longer than I've been a DMB fan. Johnny Clegg, Miriam Makeba, Hugh Masekela…all folks I've been into for a while."

"Wow, I was raised on that stuff".

"Listen, I know you have a ton of other things to do, and I'm going to get out of your hair. Just wanted to say hi, and that I hope to see you at Red Rocks and the Gorge. Any chance we can snap a quick picture together?".

"Definitely" (Dave turns to a grip and hands him my camera). I smile, ike a dipsh*t the same way I smiled when I met him at Carthage. Shake hands, and I wish him well.

Out to the car for a quick change, and I'm off to Tampa for work Tuesday. Great day. Thanks "A", I owe ya.

dreamgirls

Rashawn's mom . . .
the beautiful
Beverly ➔

*"It's very beautiful the way the sun hits your faces.
Makes me want to take y'all home and make love to ya"*

-- David J. Matthews

07.16.99 The Gorge - George, WA

Photo by David Adam Beloff

bartender 9

"Bartender you see,
this wine that's drinking me
Came from the vine that strung
Judas from the devil's tree roots
Deep deep in the ground"

10.07

bartender

bartender \ˈbär-ˌten-der\
Function: *noun*
1: a person in charge of drinks at a bar.
2: The big boss

"Bartender please,
fill my glass for me
With the wine you gave Jesus that set him free,
after three days in the ground"

SPAC August 2006

My oldest, Abigail, is a great kiddo. I took her to her first DMB show a few years ago when she was 8. She was in awe. She loves the band and their music, and I think she gets just about as much out of it as we do, although she's not as vocal about it. I also found it really interesting that she requested "Bartender", but that's her! When I was about 4 months pregnant with her I was told that she would be born with her intestines outside of her body. After her birth, they took her, medicinally paralyzed her, and waited for the swelling in her intestines to go down. It took 5 surgeries for them to finally get them all in. Once that was done, she stayed in the NICU for another month--IVs all over her (her hands, her feet, her head...). She had a broviac tube feeding straight into a major vein in her chest. She was a tough little one! Finally, one day they called me in because they were upset that she kept pulling her broviac tube out. They didn't know what to do, but I guess it bothered her, so she kept tugging at it--and she pulled it out, stitches and all! They gave up, and told me that I'd need to come in to feed her myself. I did, and eventually I got to take her home.

Then, 4 years later, she points to the scar where her broviac tube was, and she says to me,

"Mom, I have a cross on my chest."

I looked at it, and lo and behold, the scar is in the shape of a cross. She believes it's because Jesus was with her. To this day she's fine--no medical problems, and she rarely gets sick (knock on wood). I'm not a religious person. I don't go to church. If anything, I'm spiritual, and music just feeds that. As I watch her grow, I can see she's not much of a religious person either--mostly spiritual. My little doll!

So now, when I think of Bartender, I don't really think about anything religious in an institutional sense. The symbolism speaks for itself--the wine filing a glass ensuring rejuvenation; the gold being pushed aside in order to let life's true gifts bless you; the "vine that strung Judas from the devil's tree burried deep, deep in the ground" reminds us that jealousy and betrayal can run deep, but again--the wine is rejuvenating, and is symbolic of that within us that keeps us focused on cultivating our relationships and lives in an honest way. The way I see it, every belief system has symbolism like this, but this is the most familiar to us. For Abby, I think she's drawn to that symbolism, and she feels she needs to be reminded of these things throughout her life. She can't verbalize that now, but I really think kids know these things about themselves from early on! When she and I listen to the song, Dave's wailing and yelling at the end is the thing that gets us both the most (we get all teary!). I tell ya, one of the most amazing experiences was listening to that ending at Alpine, closing my eyes, feeling the energy of everyone around me and feeling the spirit of those who have passed before me--and then I look back, and I see a sea of lights coming from the audience. There's nothing like experiencing that! It's purely hypnotizing, and all I can do at that point during such moments is throw my head back, stretch out my arms, and just bathe in that energy!

I realize that I'm just part of the whole. It's like all of my energy, the energy of the audience, and the energy of the universe all connects.

At that moment, "Bartender" becomes a metaphor for what life is all about!

Antoinette
(Abigail's mom)
Germany

Photo by Jason Wagner

"I ain't promoting drinking or nothing. But whiskey comes from plants. And ya know, whatever comes from the ground has got to be good for you"
- David J. Matthews
12.28.95 Charlotte Coleseum - Charlotte, NC
Band photos by:David Adam Beloff

"Needless to say"...
Mom & Dads lock your kids in their rooms...
ban that crazy music ...
'cause these two girls are coming to a concert near you!!

These stories are all true and in the author's own words
but the names have been changed to protect
the...innocent?

Good Times!

""Melody & Missy Borrow Dad's Car"

I was laying on the beach one summer day on Long Island on my day off when I get a call from my best friend in the whole world...hmmm. Let's call her "Melody". "Leave the beach now, Missy! Immediately! I just got two 4th row tickets to see DMB in Massachusetts! We have to drive upstate to White Plains first to pick them up." Needless to say, since our cars were two pieces of crap, we stole her father's new car and were on the road racing to the show within the hour. The show was out of control and it was the closest I had ever been to Dave!! After the show ended, as we were leaving the parking lot, she smashed the car into a pole... Yes, a big bummer but nothing can get this girl down so we just sucked it up and began our 5 hour trip home to NY. To lighten up the mood we smoked a lil pot that we had saved for the way home. It wasn't too long after we left that we found ourselves being pulled over. Relaxed and not worried AT ALL, she pulls over the car and we start shoving everything illegal down our shirt and pants! Suddenly we hear shouting coming through a bullhorn! The cop is right next to us. Confused we roll down the window and he is on the loud speaker screaming "YOU DO NOT STOP IN THE RIGHT LANE"! Apparently my friend had pulled over NOT on the side of the road, but in fact in the right lane on a bridge on I-90. We start laughing hysterically and get a $200 speeding ticket. ANOTHER bummer but Melody throws it in the back of the car and we continue home. It wasn't until we got lost that our moods started to turn sour. We finally found the bridge to take us back to Long Island but couldn't seem to find the right exit. Melody looked on the left. I looked on the right. The car was a little smoky and we didn't see the cement divider. We slammed into it, crashed the car and got a flat tire. Thank God for a sweet passer-byer that changed our tire for us. So there we were driving home in her dad's smashed up new car on a spare tire, with a $200 speeding ticket in the backseat and the sun is now coming up and it's 5 in the morning. And her last words to me as I was getting out of the car,

"That was a really great show!"

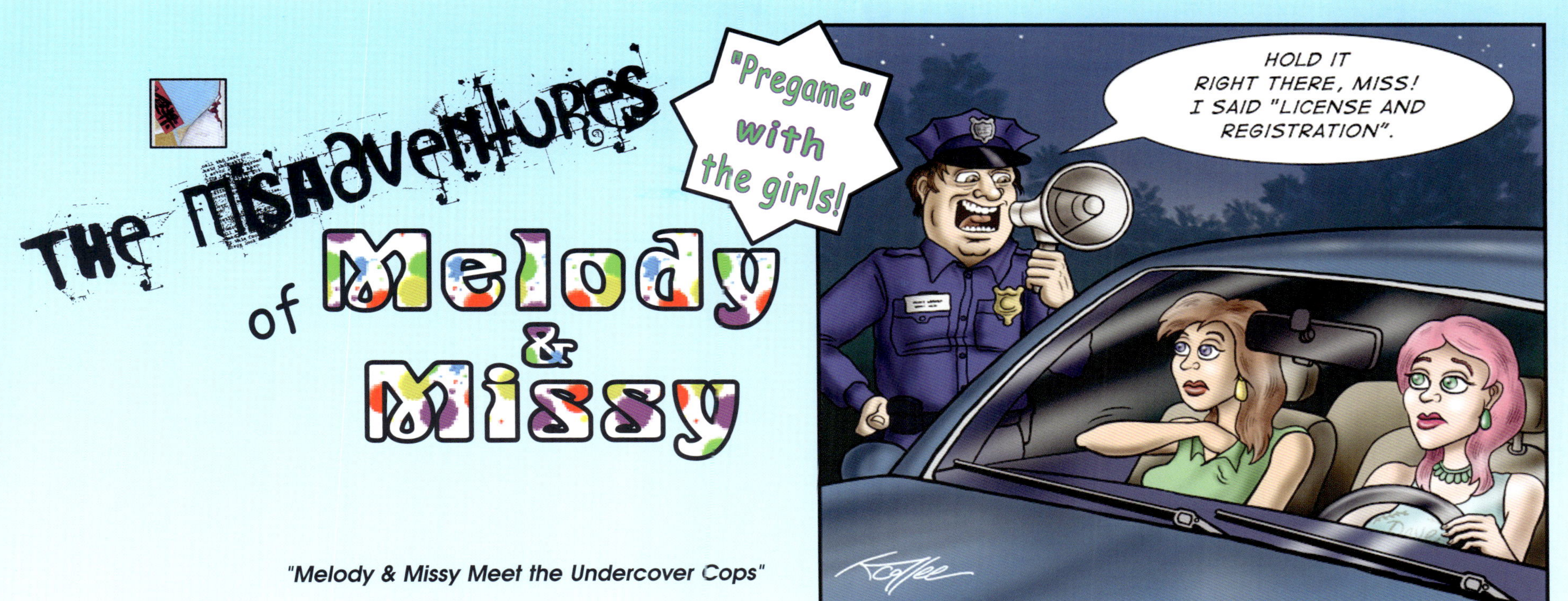

"Melody & Missy Meet the Undercover Cops"

Next show was in Hershey Park in Pennsylvania. A place I will NEVER go to again. As we were "pregaming" in the lot we were having a great time meeting people and making friends. We decided to leave our friends and go for a little stroll to see what was going on. When we returned for another beer to the car, we see 4 undercover cops dressed as fans surround the car and take our friends out and handcuff them for possession of marijuana. My friend was also put in handcuffs because it was her car and then I was soon put in handcuffs because I was 4 months short of being 21 and I was drinking. We got escorted to a paddywagan that was waiting for us. And lucky us - it was 100 degrees that day and the paddy wagon was about 170 degrees. We were taken to a holding station where we were lined up, sat in plastic lawn chairs and handcuffed to a pole. Talk about a "low point" in ur life! The cops sat across from us and dumped out all the illegal paraphernalia that was in the car. Our jaws dropped because WE HAD A LOT OF STUFF!! As the three of my friends got arrested for drugs, I was lucky enough to just get arrested for drinking. Scared and thinking it was about 46,783 hours later then it actually was, my friend and I soon find out our car wasn't impounded and we were allowed to go to the show since it hadn't even started yet!! When we returned to the car we, were greeted by such great people. They go "OMG, Missy! Melody! I cant believe what happened to you guys! Sit down. Have a beer. Have sum food". What other fans would be so welcoming besides dmb fans?? ONLY DMB FANS!!! Pissed off at what happened we find someone with weed brownies and made the best of the night! After the scared and pissed off feelings left us we had a great laugh about how we wish we could have gotten the Polcroids that the cops took of us because my friend didn't even take her sunglasses off for them!

Good times...

Photo by:Steve Speeney

If I go

Before I'm old

Oh, brother of mine

Please don't forget me if I go

10
two step

"Celebrate we will
Because life is short but sweet for certain
We climb on two by two
To be sure these days continue
These things we cannot change"

08.06

celebrate: \'se-l&-"brAt\
Function: *verb*
Etymology: Middle English, from Latin *celebratus,* past participle of *celebrare* to frequent, celebrate, from *celebr-, celeber* much frequented, famous; perhaps akin to Latin *celer*

transitive verb
1 : to live with passion, love and joy
<*celebrate* we will>
2 a : to play up for public notice

intransitive verb
1 : to observe a holiday, perform a religious ceremony, or take part in a festival

"Hey, my love,
you came to me like wine comes to this mouth
Grown tired of water all the time
You quench my heart and you quench my mind"

I was a junior at Columbine High School when all hell broke loose.

I knew both Dylan and Eric (the shooters) and six others that died. One of my best friends was Rachel Scott. At her funeral, friends and family were allowed to write their last messages to her. She had a white casket and there were black sharpie markers so that you could say whatever you wanted to her and she would be buried with the messages. I don't remember what I wrote other than a quote from the song Two Step, "Celebrate we will because life is short but sweet for certain". I thought it was really appropriate for all that we had been through and how short her life was.

Fast forward two years. I am on Nancies.org and they announce that VH1 FanClub was going to do a show on DMB. I had been wanting to tell DMB my story for a long time. In 2000 I had received a backstage pass at Mile High show but gave it to my ex boyfriend, who had introduced me to DMB.

Then I had an opportunity to meet Boyd at Bonner Springs in 2000 (actually in his dressing room!). He had donated all of his profits from a Twix commercial he did to the Columbine library fund. I had gone with a friend who had lost her brother at Columbine to thank him for his donation. I didn't get a chance to tell him my story because I felt my friend needed the time to talk more than I did.

I really just wanted to tell Dave because it was his words that I used to signify such a defining moment in my life and to put my friend to rest, forever. It was also his words that got me through a VERY rough part of my life. To this day, if I am in a bad mood or having a hard day, and every April 20, I play his music. No other lyrics or sounds have ever touched me as much as the music of the Dave Matthews Band.

So I do this online application on Nancies.org and a few weeks later I get a call from one of the producers at VH1 telling me that they wanted a video of me and family and friends etc. showing how influential DMB was in my life, and consequently, theirs. So I send that in to them as well.

The screening process took about two months or so, with the producer calling me every once in a while letting me know that I was still in their top 20/15/10 people they were interested in. Then I got the call at work that I had been one of four people chosen to be on the show out of over 10,000 applications. I jumped up and down. The feeling was incredible.

The one caveat that the producers overly emphasized was that I was NOT going to meet anyone from the band. The show was to profile only the fans and how the music affected their lives. I was alright with this because I knew that someone associated with the band or the band itself would see the show.

So fast forward to July 2001. Two producers, a camera guy and a sound guy follow me around for two full days. They filmed me at work, at home, at Rachel's grave site, at Columbine and my main interview was filmed at Red Rocks.

On July 11 they were going to film us at a WH gathering before the show in Boulder. I pull into the parking lot and the producers ask to talk with my friend Christine. I just figured they wanted to do a seperate interview with her. She walks back over with the camera guys and tells me that I was going to meet Dave right then and there. I was shocked. I had convinced myself that I was absolutely not going to meet him. Turns out that Dave found out about me and my story and told the producers that he wanted to personally invite me backstage.

I had never been more scared or nervous in my life. The build up was so incredible and now I was going to meet the man that put me here in the first place.

I walk in through the door and just saw cameras, lights and lots of people. Then I finally recognized Dave. Just standing there... and I was like yep alright there he is. I took a deep breath and just smiled at him. He walked over to me and immediately hugged me. Then I lost it. It was just too too much. I tried to talk, but the words could not come out right for the life of me. He just kept hugging me and smiling and hugging. He whispered in my ear that we could just leave all the cameras behind and that they were making him uncomfortable. So I talked and cried and talked and cried and almost made him cry and then it was over before I knew it.

Dave told me that he had to go introduce Wyclef Jean (the opener), but before he left he asked me for my phone number. A guy appeared with a pen and a piece of paper and I wrote down my home phone number. He put it in his chest pocket, hugged me again so hard and kissed me on the cheek. Then he was gone.

Oh yeah, we did talk about songs... the new album Everyday, what my favorites were and what his were. He told me that they would play Two Step for me and we talked about Bartender. He told me he thought it was the best song he had ever written. I agreed...

I have to say that the Folsom version of Bartender is one of the most intense versions I have ever seen. Anytime I put in the DVD I cry. I know he is thinking of me and Rachel. I can see it in his face, hear it in his voice... the same with Two Step. He dedicated Bartender to me, which you can hear only on the bootleg copy of the Folsom show. On the third stanza into the song before the actual lyrics, he says, "This is for my friend Sarah, say what..." or something like that.

So they played into the night, with the rain, the rainbows and then eventual darkness. I was so over stimulated I can barely remember the show...

Then the next morning I wake up late and had to get to work. I had run out of gas from the drive back home the night before, so I was waiting for AAA when the phone rang. My brother answered the phone and brought it to me. He told me that he thought it was one of my friends playing a joke on me because they said it was Dave Matthews.

So I picked up the phone... "Hello?"

"Hi this is Dave... Dave Matthews, we met last night" with his quirky southern drawl. I fell to the floor... yep this is Dave Matthews, calling me at home... right...

We talked for about 20 minutes, about the show and about me. He told me the world was in good hands if all young people were like me. Then he told me our paths would cross again. That's all I remember. I wish I had had a tape recorder or something so that I could have caught more of the conversation. I just had to keep giving myself a reality check that it was in fact Dave Matthews talking to me on the phone... The Dave Matthews!

I am very humbled right now with what a truly special experience it was. Dave... what a truly humble, gracious and good man he is! Even though he can be weird and odd in interviews I think it is because he doesn't like the attention and is kind of shy. But I guess I shouldn't speak for him.

What I do know of him is that he is a really good person with a big heart and truly cares about people. Sometimes I become a little cynical and have a lack of faith in people, but thinking of our meeting helps me renew that faith a little. I mean, c'mon he called a random chick AT HOME just because. What other rock star would do that?

Sarah Bay
Denver, Colorado

Band photo by David Adam Beloff

"We went down to Brazil, and that's a cool place. There's a lot of cool places south of the border to hang out, I tell ya. We need to open up all the borders and people and just all hang out together and dance. They got some good tunes down there, too, and there should be a lot more movement, there should be a lot more hangin' out going on, we should all be dancin' and chillin' and goin' crazy."
- David J. Matthews
01.29.99 Landmark Theater - Syracusse, NY
Miller's
Dave Matthews Band
Carter
Dave
Leroi
Boyd
Stefan

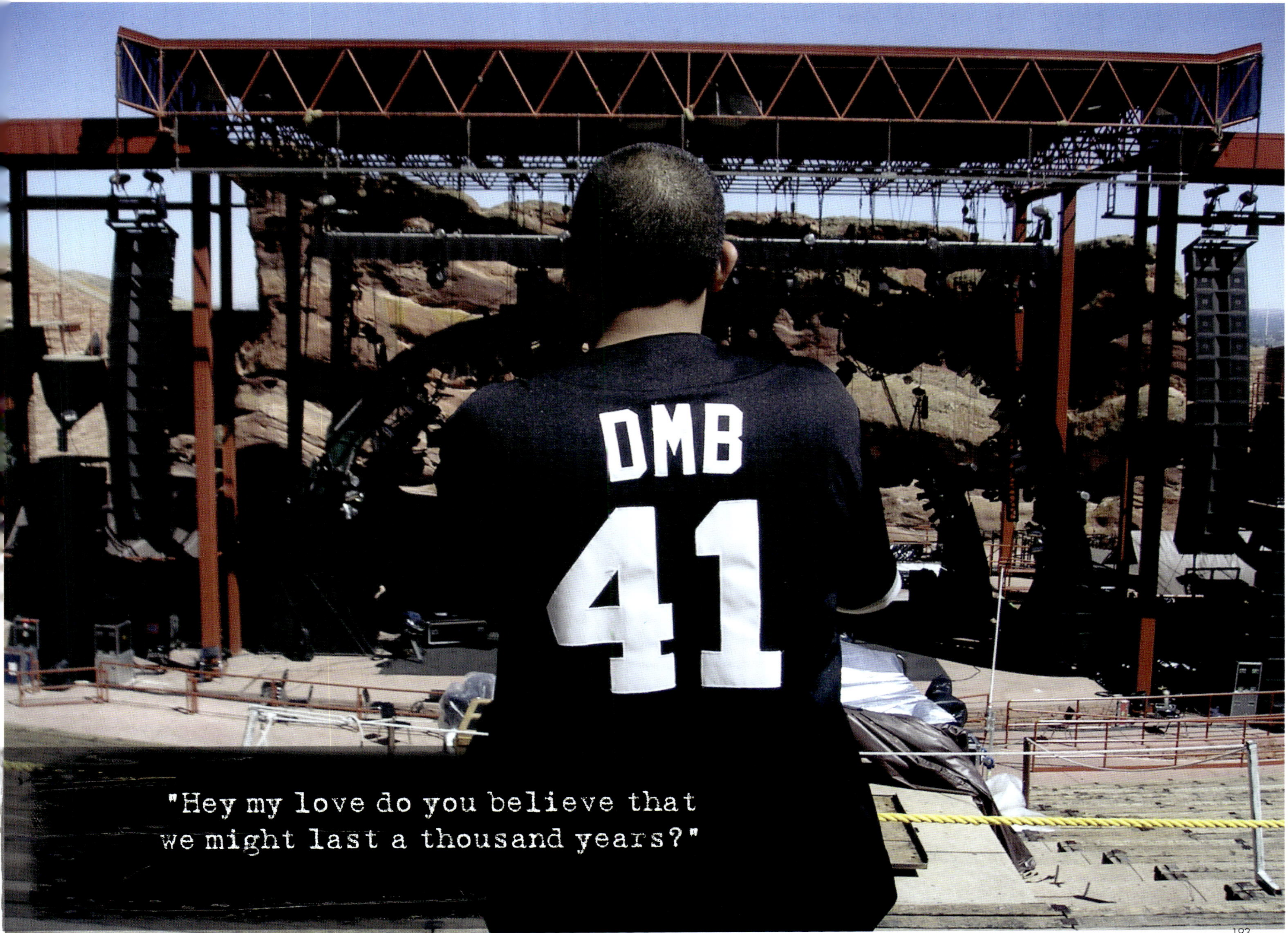

"Hey my love do you believe that
we might last a thousand years?"

Photo by Ben Sokolowski

DAVE MATTHEWS BAND
99
ACOUSTIC TOUR
daveMatthewsband
DAVE MATTHEWS BAND
DAVE MATTHEWS BAND
2002 TOUR
BUSTED STUFF
DAVE MATTHEWS BAND
CENTRAL PARK NYC 09.24.2003
BOSTON
DAVE MATTHEWS BAND
FOXBORO STADIUM
JUNE 16-17 2001
DAVE & TIM
HEADWATERS BENEFIT
I ♥ DMB
Dave Matthews
Tim Reynolds
DAVE MATTHEWS BAND
WORLD TOUR
Dave Matthews Band
Minarets.net
dave matthews band
DMB
ONE SWEET WHIRLED
DAVE MATTHEWS BAND
The love of my life Sarah Grace

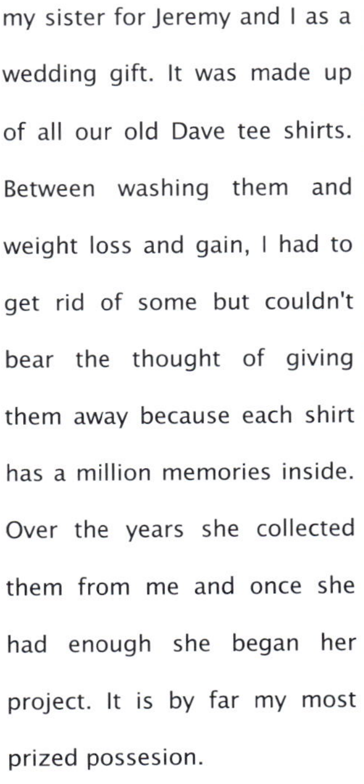

The quilt was made by my sister for Jeremy and I as a wedding gift. It was made up of all our old Dave tee shirts. Between washing them and weight loss and gain, I had to get rid of some but couldn't bear the thought of giving them away because each shirt has a million memories inside. Over the years she collected them from me and once she had enough she began her project. It is by far my most prized possesion.

Amy

Photo by Jenn Berry

Ants...SPAC '06 Night 1

Photo by Justin Pagliuco

Celebrate we will!

epilogue 11

A SHORT STORY
A CODE
A CONTEST

THE DAVE-NCI CODE

JEREMY CANNON

A short story...a code...a contest...?

Imagine, if you will, a place where all may not be what it seems.

A place where one man's dreams meet his music.

Our hero is ready for a change . . . ready to solve the puzzle of his life.

Your puzzle is to find the secret embedded code that is hidden in his story.

Hints? There are none - at least not yet.

Where to start? Why, where all stories start . . . at the beginning.

For additional information and rules, visit www.LJMSart.com

He wakes up

in the morning,

does his teeth,

bite to eat,

and

he's rolling,

never changes

a thing.

It was just after six in the morning when the light started to filter in through the window. He knew that at any moment the alarm would be going off and he would have to get up and begin again. Come to think of it, it seemed like his life had become one continuous never ending cycle of the same thing. Getting up in the morning to run, followed by work, and then home again. He sometimes wondered to himself why, And furthermore would this life ever lead anywhere. Was he becoming the person he had always wanted to be? As he began to slowly rise from his bed these thoughts that had seemed to plague him had momentarily disappeared. He could see through his window that it would be a nice day outside. It made him happy to see that at least the weather was going to cooperate. He allowed himself to smile a little. He always said to himself that today "I will try to do the best that I can at whatever I am doing." Sometimes with the trials of life weighing heavily on him, this saying was easier said than done. He got up and this action caused him to swear. He thought that maybe he could just lay back down for another half hour. He would get a good start with just another half hour of sleep. He smirked, knowing that this ongoing mental debate that was waged every morning by him would end the same way it did everyday. With him begrudgingly getting dressed and going out for his morning run. With a heavy sigh, he put on his clothes and running shoes. Fully dressed, he was ready to go now. The only thing missing from his running ensemble was his mp3 player. He considered this his most important item to have on a run. Not only did the music keep him going, it also allowed him to forget his troubles. "I'm going to have to find that thing before I leave," he thought to himself. Since he bought it there was really only one band that he ever had in there. The Dave Matthews Band was his favorite band, and were playing all the time. He really didn't even listen to any other music. He had never stopped to think about it. He had been listening to them for so long he didn't remember a period of not listening to them. What time did he have to be at work today, he wondered. Thinking about his favorite band made him temporarily forget about work. It usually did. It also made him forget about his troubles and pretty much anything he wanted to forget. "I had better get going," he thought, as he looked at the clock again. It was funny to him how in the morning time seemed to move much faster when you needed to be somewhere at a certain time. He was against the clock as far as time went today. He had things to do and not enough time to do it in. So he feverishly began to search for his mp3 player. It had to be close. "Where the hell is my music?" he wondered aloud. Out of the corner of his eye he saw a speck of blue sticking out from under a shirt, and knew that he had found what he was looking for. He grabbed it and he felt troubles melting away. As he held his mp3 player aloft as if it were some kind of golden treasure he did something that he had been waiting to do since his search began: he pressed play. The familiar music surrounded him. "I'm going to have a great day today," he said. It was funny how the first few chords of a Dave Matthews Band song could change someone's thoughts so quickly. But their music seemed to do that for him. But now coming to the front door he was ready to venture outside. As he made it outside the song "Ants Marching" began to play. The music that was playing seemed to match what was going on sometimes. He knew that starting out slow with running long distances was the idea. Along with listening to his favorite music, he would be just fine. The mp3 player was his constant companion. It was with him on trips going to work and coming home from work but it didn't matter where he was, the music was with him. "He wakes up in the morning, does his teeth, bite to eat, and he's rolling, never changes a thing." These words really made him feel like he was really speeding his day up, because once he listened to these particular lyrics, it seemed as if his day was truly beginning. So here he was, ready to go. Once again set for a morning run. It seemed every morning he would do everything he could to prolong that first step. Because after that he was going. No stopping, no going back to sleep, his day was beginning. He walked up to the starting point. He was a little annoyed that he said "You need to do this," to himself all the time. Not like he needed to remind himself where he was ten years ago. As the music played on he flashed back to a time when he was in college. Could he wish himself back to this time in life for him? Would he even want to? As the flashback continued he saw himself as he was truly for the first time. He was a mess. Looking at himself during those times was a humbling experience. He thought he had everything at the time. But he could see now that he was lost and really had no plan for life. He might have been having fun at the time. He was doing a little dance. And laughing. He was probably having the best of times. He knew that the next day he would wake up and not remember where he had been or what he had been doing. He would start this process all over and continue to think that this is what college was for. However, he knew he was fooling himself, because his partying had gotten in the way of everything, even school. The reason he was there was to get an education. Yet while he was having the time of his life, he was unaware that he was just becoming a statistic. This last part of the memory brought him back to the present. He was standing there, not knowing how much time passed. "I'm going to do better today," he said to himself. He couldn't believe he had messed up so bad in college. He had many opportunities presented to him and threw them all away. It was hard to think about himself being in college. So he decided to think about the present instead. He was still standing at the starting line as "Ants Marching" played on. "Lights down, you up and die." This lyric was enough to get him going. He was taking the first step. And he was off. It seemed most days it took a lot of mental convincing to get to this point, yet he always ended up running. He knew how good it was for him. Also being mostly in front of people as far as starting his day with a long distance run would make everything else that he did seem easy. So he was a few steps into his run when he could tell that it would be about the wav he wanted it to be.

His body responded well to the first few steps and he knew that everything was going to be o.k. Most times he was able to spot any problems right off. He was waiting to play his favorite song for when he really got tired. All of the songs kept him motivated, yet some of them really got him going. He had made a CD of some of his favorite songs, and he played them mostly on his runs. He found that hearing some of his favorites back to back made him forget he was running in the first place. "Good," he thought to himself as "Tripping Billies" started playing. This song made him really very happy. Time to turn up the volume and sing. He always laughed to himself at this point because he had gotten past the initial tiredness and now he was out here doing something good for himself. As good as running feels or is for a person it is also a great escape and time alone. No matter how many great friends you have or how much you accomplish, alone time is important for a person. No matter if you have gone on and won a race, which he wishes he could do or whether you are trying to win at life, everyone needs alone time. He always wondered whether other people thought as he did. He thought that many people probably did a little, but maybe not as much. He had wondered why his thoughts would drift to times gone by instead of on the task at hand. But then he thought that maybe that is the connection he had with running. Running allowed all the thoughts to present themselves in his mind. And then as quickly as they appear they are gone. Allowing him to think about some things for a short period of time. He saw this as a good thing because most people's difficulty dealing with problems was taking too long to decide what to do. As he thought this last thought he heard the lyrics in Tripping Billies that made him smile.

These were lyrics that made him smile because he had what is considered by him a smart, loyal group of friends. The lyrics were "you and me and all our friends, such a happy human race." Half the people he thought of when he heard these lyrics he knew would never be coming here. They existed on a computer screen from all points over the United States. But it was they thought like him about the Dave Matthews Band that counted to him. He had sometimes thought about how many people that were here who felt the same way he did about the band. Ever since the first time he heard them he knew somehow that he would be a fan for life. He thought now about that first time hearing them and said "I have to tell everyone I know about them." He had done that ever since though not everyone always wanted to hear about them. The unfortunate ones he called them. He smirked to himself at this description. "They will believe, they will." He allowed himself to laugh out loud at his own humor. Everytime he listened to their music he just didn't get how people could not think they were the greatest band ever. He would just shrug his shoulders and usually go on with what he was doing. But then it would creep back into his mind and he would start to wonder how someone could not like them. Check that, love them. He smiled again knowing that not everyone felt that in the same way that he did. But that was o.k. He then realized that while he had been thinking about all of these random things that some of his run was over. It was always good to get some of this run over without realizing it, or forgetting that you were even exerting yourself. He flashed back to the present now and he was starting to feel a bit tired. It was, in fact, a very nice day outside and the way for him to get back to his house was on this road. There were no shortcuts. Chandler Boulevard was a long road and it provided a challenge to him. He hadn't gone that long as far as the run was, and he knew that he had a long way to go. But then he started to think about this in terms in life. There were no shortcuts and sometimes you have to do things you didn't like to do to help find your own way. At this moment he flashed back to a time when he was younger and his mother would try to show him the way to live. He thought she was such a great person and without her guidance my life would be drastically different. He thought about all the dumb things he had done during his lifetime and how she had always been there no matter what. It amazed him that she was such a strong person. On his own, he would have been lost a long time ago, but due to her loyalty and love for him he felt an appreciation for her that laid dormant for way too long. No other person had made him feel the same way he did about her. He never really realized it. She was great to him, as far as he was concerned. The person he wanted to be most like. At this point he came back to the present. On his way out of the door he had not really felt like running, but now that he was about a quarter of the way through he felt good and thinking about things certainly helped him pass the time. Looking ahead he thought that I am only this far, but that's o.k. I feel good so far. He stared ahead and saw nothing but the path in front of him. But he thought about all the things that he had pondered on and knew he won't be able to quit thinking. When he runs the thoughts just appear, whether he wants them to or not. So he just figured that he should push on and see what comes to him. As he was running, he could tell the next song by the very first cymbal sound. It was "Grey Street". Also another one of his favorites. This song was one that made him sing out loud, but all of them did that. So then he said silently, " You gotta sing, man." Which made him smile again. You have to have a sense of humor if you are going to run long distances. Being out on the road this long can make a person bored, he thought to himself. To be out here this long is quite and accomplishment. "Most people would of given up by now," he told himself. It was things like this that he said to himself to keep him going. To have this ability to really stay in this mood would be great, he thought. He wished that he could be in this mood all the time. The endorphins were kicking in and he truly felt good. Even singing out loud wasn't something he did normally now, but he didn't care. He was feeling good despite feeling like a sweaty mess. He started to flashback to all the good times he had and realized that maybe it wasn't as bad as he thought. "You know," he said "somehow I'm realizing that I am the only one who can make myself feel better." "I can't leave that up to anyone else." There were many times that he could remember that were really fun for him. He thought of times when coming home seemed to be the last thing he wanted to do. So many good times. His mind thought back to times in college that he would never forget. Times that were worth the wasted years. But to him it was to much of the bad that outweighed the good. As quickly as the good memories were there they were gone. How quickly his mind had switched from feeling very good to anxious about his future.

Again he wondered if he would much rather be someone else. "Could I have been anyone other than me?" he wondered. He wished that he would have made different choices in life. He had plenty of opportunities. Only he didn't take advantage of them. He always wanted more from life than he had. Not necessarily material things, but more peace of mind, more plans for life. Would he become the person he wanted to be? This thought had been with him for a long time. "Will anyone see me as I want them to?" These questions crept through his mind every now and again. He didn't like thinking these thoughts, but they seemed to appear from time to time. He tried to shake these bad thoughts from his mind all the time. It seemed like running helped him to clear his mind of them. He looked up and realized that he was almost halfway through his run. Not quite, but almost. Which was good enough for him. He had looked at the buildings along the route that he had taken. They marked his progress for him because he had ran this route many times. It seems like when he first started running he would struggle past these buildings. He had known once he had got past a certain building he was that much closer to finishing. But it seems like the buildings used to mock him. Almost as if they knew how exhausted he was. They almost seemed to enjoy watching him the whole time as he struggled mightily. That was a long time ago. Now as he had grown stronger and more confident the buildings almost seemed to bow as he speeded by. It was as if the buildings had been old ghosts who had gone from scary to respectful in a matter of months. He wondered if this was even possible. Why would he even have this thought inside of his brain? It was like this thought process had really just now come to him. But in the back of his mind he knew he always thought about things like this. To him, almost everything had a purpose, or a feeling to it. As he continued on running he knew that the road back would lead past the same buildings and probably the same thoughts. He sometimes thought about himself running, thinking these things, while everyone else was in such a big hurry to go to their jobs or home. As these thoughts were reeling in him he focused on getting to the halfway point of his run. Although getting to the halfway point was an accomplishment there was still much more to go. But at least he would be halfway done. He could be in Arizona, where he currently was, or anyone else in the world, but running and thinking were two things that he had found a kinship with. It was his private time to really collect his thoughts and get his brain working. "You think too much," he said as if talking to another person. He smiled again, repeating what other people had told him before. He just couldn't help it. As he approached the familiar streets that marked the halfway point coming up now, he started to speed up. Getting to that halfway point was only seconds away and he could start to feel the break that was coming his way. At the halfway point he always walked for a couple minutes. He knew what was coming, and a break would feel great. As he reached that halfway point and slowed to a walk he could feel all the sweat that seemed to have been held back pour down his face. He had always thought if it wasn't for all the sweat and pure exhaustion it caused that running would be a great time. As he breathed deeply and tried to catch his breath he let the words of the song that was playing soak in. "They came down crushing, remember when I used to play for all the loneliness that nobody notices now." It was in the middle of the song "#41". It was his favorite Dave Matthews Band song, and it all seemed like it came at a perfect time. It was halfway through the song, and he was halfway through his run. This song really meant something to him. He almost felt like he could write a story based on this song. He continued walking down the street, still trying to catch his breath listening to his favorite song. As the music melodically played on, he thought to the other day when he received a phone call from a family member. This call was kind of crushing to him. He had learned that a family member that he loved very much had relapsed into trouble. It was something that was said in passing, but it made him hurt inside. He said nothing of it, but he would remember good times with this person and how great of a person this was. He wasn't even mad, just disappointed. But at the same time he was thinking of this person, he thought more strongly of how much he cared. Like when he used to play catch with this person and just laugh and have a great time with this person. And for the first time in a while, a light clicked on inside of him. He said to himself that "if I can look at the positive aspects of things my life will be enhanced." He didn't know if these were the endorphins kicking in or him just trying to look at things in a more positive light, but he was always used to looking at things with a glass half empty attitude. It was like a light had clicked on for the first time in a long time. That one little change in thought had changed his narrow view on success. Also to make things better he also thought about going home in a few months.

He flashed back to the times right before he had moved away when he was back with his family. He was indifferent to their wishes. He would play around with his life, and he would expect other people to clean up the mess for him. When they wouldn't do it, their would be arguments. How he wished he could go back in time. As he walked he looked for the song "The Best of What's Around." If any other song reminded him of being a good person and listening to other people's ideas, and not caring where you are, but who you are with, then that was it. Of all the songs, that one spoke to him the most now. It was funny to him how this great music that he had listened to for fifteen years had also taught him so many things. It was as if each CD of the Dave Matthews Band was a road map for life. He felt like this lots concerning the band, yet everytime was like a new experience. He smiled as he walked back to the halfway point. He had a smile and the nice thing about it was that it was genuine. It seemed like most of his smiles had been genuine, but deep inside their was a great sadness. The last ten years had been filled with bits of disappointment and some lonliness. It seemed like most of the decisions that he had made had been the wrong ones. But now as he got ready to run back to his house he wondered if all of the wrong decisions had prepared him for that which was ahead. This little thought caught him because what if a wrong decision became something useful. Just as he pondered this the song "Pig" started to play. If was as if someone was sending him a signal. Even though nobody was around, he asked "are you messing with me right now?" It seemed as if sometimes when he asked a question his mp3 player would go to the right song that would help him. The part of the song he notices the most says "there's bad times, but that's o.k., we just look for love in here." He knows that sometimes he had trouble getting past the bad times. But getting past that and appreciating life, or just being fortunate right now to have a life was all he was thinking about. He remembered back over all the troubling times he had and remembered how he had always landed on his feet. As these thoughts ran through his mind "Pig" played on. "I'm doing better than what I thought I was. He knew that soon his life would be swept away and he had better take advantage of the time he had. One thing that he noticed was that people were always almost begging for more time at the end. Some of the people will have regrets at the end. Our lives are not guaranteed to last a certain amount of time. Nobody knows how long they will be around. Whether people live life slow or fast, their time is coming. And it was at this moment that his body had this incredible surge of energy. It seemed as though his mind was waiting for this change of heart. A time that he thought that "I'm wasting my time worrying about things in the past." At that moment it seemed as though all worries and doubts had been released. It was like he was a new person. Looking at everything for the first time with views coming from a different perspective. Everything felt different now. He had this incredible amount of energy and things seemed to look a little different. Instead of imposing and frightening, things appeared to be inviting and friendly. It was almost like being here in this moment had totally changed his point of view. Fears and doubts had been replaced by hope and happiness. In all his joy and his new happiness he had forgotten where he was. He was still here standing, he only was halfway done. "Damn," he muttered. He rolled his eyes. It was a funny moment. With all his happiness he had forgotten that he was standing five miles away from his house. He had done this run a million times. Waiting here any longer would only prolong it, so he took the first step back as "Grace Is Gone" started to play. He thought this was a rather ironic song to be playing right now as well. He smiled and thought "I know this is more than coincidence." It had been a while since he had a real relationship. Not because he couldn't, just out of choice. His last relationship had its difficulties, and after that he gave up. But now he wanted to try again. The prospect of dating again seemed inviting instead of daunting. He tried to think of all the qualifications he most admired in prospective girlfriends. Then a small smile broke through. He knew what it was he wanted. To any other person who knew him it was obvious what he was searching for. A girl who into the Dave Matthews Band as much as he was. It was so obvious to him right now. As another song he loved, "Stay", started to play he thought about how simple it all was. Because to him a girl who liked the Dave Matthews Band as much as him told him all he needed to know about her. In his convinced mind thought, "I have made this way too difficult." It was very simple and he realized now instead of thinking about his past he had shifted his focus onto the bright future. It was nice to think about what was to come. He wanted to continue to focus on the future. He realized that for so long he had focused on the negative, while all the time he should have been focusing on the positive. But none of this mattered now.

All that mattered to him now was the realization of it. At least if you realize it than you can do something about it. All of these thoughts again had made him forget how tired he was. Sweat was pouring down his face now, play time was over and the last half of the run was work. He did enjoy this exercise, but it was stressful at times. He always had to make sure he had drank plenty of water before. He started to struggle. "I can finish this," he thought. After all the realizations he had today he was not quitting on this run. He had come out plenty of times unprepared and learned the hard way how preperation was so important. All he had wanted was to get through this run and put all his new knowledge into practice. It was getting better as the time wore on. He knew that him stopping at all would only cause him to be out here longer. And to be out here any longer than necessary was not a good thing. So he pushed on. And as he was running along gaining a little momentum, he now had realized how his last couple of thoughts all translated to life. Love had seemed to enter him finally and all the worries of the world seemed to go away. All his thoughts seemed to focus on things that he could control and away from the things he couldn't. "If only I put you in my mind earlier" he thought speaking of the positive thoughts that he had gained today. Now he was thinking that they were there all along, just buried. He felt that sadly most people had probably had these postive thoughts I'm having right now washed away by some unforeseen events in life. How sad that most people give up after only a couple setbacks. He was guilty of this. He himself had given up on really trying to do great things only to give up way too soon. How many things had passed him by that he had an opportunity for but he had already given up. That was not important to him anymore. What was important was the present and what this meant to him was what he could control from now on would be positive. What was done was done. As he focused back into the present and begin to look around he realized that he was nearly three quarters done. Far enough away to not feel like he was done, yet close enough where he could feel the end coming. Today seemed to be such a big day. It had all started the usual way, but through a change in thinking and a different attitude he knew today was different. No longer would he let his past dictate his future. When he had realized he had been doing this for a long time it seemed so unnecessary. Each day is given as only so long. We only have so long to be here, and we might as well make the most of it. He thought back to all the times he considered not so good and realized that he had learned from them. Tomorrow is going to be a great day also. He had never quite thought like this before. He had always looked to the next day with trepidation and fear of the unknown. But now he had known that his good thoughts leads the way. This was comforting to him. He was now about three quarters of the way done and all of his good thoughts were flooding his mind. He wanted to tell so many people how much he cared about them the way he never had. It's funny how he had passed on so many chances to tell the people close to him how he felt. But he never had, and he never knew why. Now he knew after this there were way too many people that he had not told. People who had helped him out in the past, people who had been around him a long time. But he still had time to do that. It was very important to him. "I'm going to tell them now. Better late than never had not been truer to him than that moment. Taking advantage of the time given was something he wanted to focus on. He used to think that some days were never coming to an end. But as he looked up and saw exactly how much running he had left to do he realized the shortness of time and the finality of it. As he looked up he started to notice his surroundings. waltzing around with things in nature. The backdrop of his surroundings were something that he had come to appreciate as part of nature's. Sometimes with all that is going that is going on in life, we lose focus on things that back some time ago were looked at with great reverence and respect. But with people as busy as they are now, some things take a back seat. When he focused on the mountains and things that surrounded him, all the cars and all the other distractions seemed to disappear. He was really happy for the first time in a while and he knew that something had changed. Looking up again he knew that he was close. Being done with this run meant moving up the road and that is exactly what he was doing. Somewhere along the line he had gone from tired to exhausted. He always got this way near this point. But he never gave up. It was about this point into it that he went on autopilot. He had reached the point now where he never quit running until he was finished. He then flashed back to various times in the past when he was in a position to succeed. "Hey, your screwing this up" said one person. "You've got to do better" said another. Yet another said, "We just can't keep you on here."

If he had thought of these situations before he would dwell on lost chances. Only now his head was clear and this time instead of seeing these as lost opportunities he saw them as things that happened. That was it. Nothing more, nothing less. This was a nice change for him. Instead on focusing on negatives he would please his mind by thinking positive thoughts. He was starting to get near the point where he knew he was almost done. There were just a few more streets to go. He knew that his focus had shifted. He thought "Life's better when I concentrate on things that I can control." With about a fourth of the run left, he started to go over in his mind all of the days thoughts. He had gotten up today with the attitude that he wouldn't wish this life on anyone. It had become a never ending cycle of the same thing day after day. He had lost hope that things were going to ever be any better a long time ago. He had taken a pass many times on when or where it all went wrong, only knowing that somewhere along the line something had gone wrong. He had started today just like every other day, rising early to run, followed by his job. Everyday like this had put hope further out of his mind. But today was different. All of these realizations came to him today. While running today he had started thinking about where his life was going and which direction it was headed? But by asking himself these questions he discovered other things. He now knew that even though he wasn't exactly where he wanted to be right now he would get there. It wasn't important that life hadn't turned out exactly as he planned. "I can change that," he thought. "All I have to do is make the most of everyday." He also looked back at all the memories that he considered bad and realized that he had, quite honestly, learned from those experiences. He would be able to finally let things go. It felt like a huge weight had been lifted off of him. He felt lighter as he came down the last part of his run. He was sweating heavily now, but he could take much more now due to the fact it felt like his whole life had changed. He was flipping through his mp3 player to find just the perfect song for this ending to his run. He felt better today than at any other time. He needed something that would allow him to end this run on a high note. So he flipped through and found the song. It was mellow, but what he needed at the time. It was a song that's more than good for right now. It was the Central Park version of Jimi Thing. The familiar music started and the first few words were being sung. "Lately I've been feeling low, a remedy is what I'm seeking." He relaxed more than before as this song usually made him do. His mind started to wonder to wondrous places. He started to think about how much this music meant to him. He had always liked music and found it to be relaxing. But what this music had done was capture his feelings in musical form. But not just in one song. Every song was like this. He used to wonder if he was the only one who felt like this. But he knew what sort of people had felt the same way that he did. All kinds of people from all over the world had been touched by this bands music. It had effected all kinds of people in different ways. For some the music of the Dave Matthews Band was a release from everyday life. To others it represented different cultures coming together to make great music. Still to others it was a great combination of different elements to make beautiful melodies. Here was a man, running along towards the stopping point. He was enjoying their music as he ran along. He, like everyone else, was getting something out of their music. He knew that he had always listened to them. Where he goes, their music goes. He knew that. But as all of these realizations about life hit him today he thought of how the music of the Dave Matthews Band had always been there. He thought of how the lyrics of most of the songs by Dave Matthews had really made him think. In fact his thoughts today had started when he first started playing the music. He knew that listening to their music had made him feel better, but today he felt connected. He said "I have been listening to the band for so long, but today more than ever, the music really speaks to me." He smiled knowing that many other people have probably had that same experience that he had today. Knowing that he will continue to listen to their music and learn as he goes along were two things that he looked forward to. Looking ahead at the horizon he could see the final street coming up. He was truly happy today. He would bring all that he could from now on and not take anything for granted. He would take advantage of his opportunities from now on. Everyone makes mistakes, but it is what you learn from them that is important. He need some water pretty soon, and he was thinking about that first drink when he got back. He knew how satisfying it would be and was feeling the same way about his future. He was looking forward to getting done with this run. Why did he wait so long to really do something about his outlook. It didn't really matter that he had waited so long to do something, it only mattered that he did. And this was the point to him.

If you won't do anything to change problems you don't like then the fault becomes your own. But if you have chosen to do something, the change may not even happen when you want it to, but it will happen. The decision for you to do something is the most important. As this last thought crossed his mind the finish line was only a few feet away. He could feel the endorphins kicking in. He started the final push. If he had really been ever glad to see the complex that he lived in appearing it was now. He always felt this way at this point. No matter how much his mind was thinking something else the last few feet made him think of exhaustion. Be careful, he thought. He had seen many people hurt themselves on the last few feet of runs. He wanted to make sure that he ended this on a good note. So he slowed his pace a bit. He sure was glad that he had decided to run today. What a day it had been. A day of growth, realizations and discovery. He was thinking back to the morning when he first woke up when going back to bed was something where it would have changed the whole day. It was funny to him that some small decisions could make such a big difference. It was related to his small change of attitude today. He was really hot. So hot that the pavement melts. But he pushed on and crossed the finish line. It was an line that was right in front of his complex. It was the same place where he had started from. He smiled as he crossed the line. He walked into the parking lot of the complex, breathing heavily, sweating profusely. It was probably around 8:40 a.m. he guessed, but it was still very hot, even this early. He slowly walked through the parking lot trying to catch his breath. His wonder at all of this that had occurred today was running through his mind. His heart was beating so fast, the sweat was pouring down his face rapidly. His clothes were drenched with sweat. He was trying to catch his breath. "I have to get inside and get some water," he thought. He had run this far almost everyday for the past couple months, yet he was always this tired. It took such a huge toll on him physically, but when it came to mentally, it helped him immensely. He knew that eventually the endorphins would overtake him and his mood would elevate. But today he knew that he didn't need the endorphins to feel better. He already discovered that his own way in through his mind was internal. He had the power to make himself feel better. No external source could do that. "Well," he thought "maybe one." He now looked down at the tiny blue mp3 player in his hand. He was praying that they made music forever. He always knew how important this music was to him, and now he realized how important it really had been to him. He felt like he always had a very strong connection to it. He for certain reasons knew why he had always been drawn to it. It was and always had been good music. But was their something more to it? Did this music steer his life from the wrong side to the right side? "You never know," he thought. He also made the double meaning reference to the song of the same name. Because you do never know about things, or the way things are going to be or the way things are ending and why. But to carry on with a good attitude and to be prepared for anything that comes your way with positivity is the way to be. Because you never know. Dwelling on past mistakes doesn't do any good and most likely won't help you move on. He thought about how fortunate he was to have all that he had. Some people didn't have what he had. So for him to worry about small things was trivial. Maybe helping others was his calling. "You could do that, he answered to himself. He was still walking through his large complex. As he passed through the complex he saw families together. The little kids running around. People laughing, having fun, being together. Getting down with his run was an accomplishment that he was proud of. But as Dreaming Tree was playing on in the background, he thought of someone that he really needed to talk to. He was starting to walk a little faster now. He was in a hurry. He was going to do something that was long overdue. He was walking through the complex and the sun was hot on his head and back. He finally reached his door and stuck the key into the lock. The lock turned and the cold air blasted him in the face. It felt like the coldest he had ever felt. He automatically went from really hot to really cold. The sweat had instantly dried. It was like walking in from rain right into a dry place. He set his mp3 down, turning off his music for the first time in nearly two hours. He next headed to the fridge, where the cold water waited patiently for him. He opened the fridge and it seemed to have a glow around it. This is what it seemed like to him, even though it was probably because he was so dehydrated. He grabbed the water. His dog was at his feet. His dog wanted to play. He bent down to pet his dog, and walked into his room. He tried to take his wet clothes off. He had trouble getting his shirt off, he forgot how hard it was to get wet clothes off. He could let the sweat dry, but he had other things to do today.

All Manga by GIO !

He stumbled around the room trying to get this shirt off. He thought how comical this would be if someone else were here. But it was only him and the dog. "I'm glad it's only you here, Sheena," he said. The dog looked at his with indifference and yawned. This was funny to him. He started to laugh. He didn't know why, but it was very funny. Laughing so hard tears started to roll down his face. After he quit laughing he grabbed the water and drank it. The water was nice and cold and he gulped it down. He was drinking it so fast that the water was going to splash all over, but he didn't care. It will dry pretty soon he thought. When he got all the water he wanted he went back into the kitchen and put the water back. He shut the refrigerator door and knew that all he wanted to do now was find his phone. He went back into his room and found the charger. He pulled on the cord until he found the charger. He pulled on the cord until the phone appeared. Now finally over the tiredness of the run he dialed. It rang a couple times before she picked up. "Hello," she said. "Hey," it's me", he replied. "Hi, Jeremy" she said. "Mom, I just wanted to tell you how much I really appreciate you and how much I love you." And this one act he knew he was finally becoming the person he had always wanted to be.

So, did you see it?
Can you figure it out?

How well do you
know the music?

There is a code . . .
A special DMB message embedded in the story.
For contest rules and prizes, visit www. LJMSart.com

The Begatitudes
by Mary Warner

So-and-so begat thus-and-such begat this-and-that begat thus-and-so. We humans, we begat like exuberant bunnies, we do, but not simply in a biological sense. Our minds are too active, our hands and legs too twitchy to limit ourselves to mere "Sperm, meet Egg" procreation. There's more to be done, by golly. We must create on other levels. It's imperative.

Art, science, music, economics, literature, ad nauseum infinitum. There's nothing we chain of traveling monkeys won't touch, won't attempt. And after we are through begetting a particular creation, it breathes a life of its own, the begotten becoming the begetter in our stead. A non-human lineage is born and reproduces, with some creations, like biological entities, producing at a more prolific rate than others. Poe's "The Raven," Darwin's Theory of Natural Selection, "The Inner Classic of the Yellow Emperor," Picasso's cubism, Audubon's birds, Einstein's Theory of Relativity, Munch's "The Scream," Michelangelo's "David." Each of these works has spawned countless others. Add your personal favorites to the list. They're seminal works and society knows it, practically agrees in unison for a change, although not necessarily upon birth. Sometimes it takes convincing to make people see the value in the ugly, unfamiliar baby that will go on to inspire great begetting.

Not always, though. Sometimes, the baby is beautiful upon earthly entry, kissed by Ms. Universe prior to delivery. The begotten is immediately accepted for its quality, its relevance, its gong-resounding effect on our hearts.

If the creator is especially adept at begetting, and his many works show a constancy of quality, along with longevity in relevance, it's quite possible that Ms. Universe has also bestowed Muse status on him, ensuring much future begetting. (And you thought Muses were the musty stuff of Greek myth or the ladies of diaphanous costume in Xanadu. P'shaw!) Achieving Muse status it not a thing an individual in the traveling monkey chain can willfully accomplish. It happens quite in spite of any special efforts, and may not even be wanted by the begetter. It's such a burden to be a Muse, what with all that responsibility for inspiration. Not to worry. The Muse must only beget, and the begotten will take care of the rest.

Could there be Muses lurking among us in this present age? Most surely, but that longevity of relevance can be a stickler. As History shakes her skirts, and the dust settles beneath her feet, certainly she will see that Dave Matthews Band was one of the entities kissed by Ms. Universe. How will she know? By counting up all the begotten the band's music has sired.

Blessed are the begetters, for their work shall live on in the begotten.
Blessed are the begotten, for they shall be tomorrow's begetters.

useful websites

DMB FANSITES/FORUMS
http://amidreaming.org
http://www.andwedanceaway.com/forum/
http://www.angelfire.com/mb2/DMB/
http://www.antsmarching.org
http://www.cornerofgrey-street.com
http://www.dmb.crush-me.net
http://www.dmbftp.net
http://www.dmbgame.com/
http://www.dmbrr.com
http://www.dmbfans.info
http://www.dmbfansite.com
http://www.dontburnthepig.org
http://www.geocities.com/whatwouldyousay36/
http://kitkatjam.com/
http://www.liog.org
http://members.tripod.com/~dancinnanci/dmbpage.html
http://www.myspace.com/markmend12
http://www.nancies.org
http://www.thesedayscontinue.org
http://www.weeklydavespeak.com

OFFICIAL DMB SITES
http://www.davematthewsband.com
http://www.warehouse.davematthewsband.com
http://stores.musictoday.com/store/default.asp?band_id=1
http://road.davematthewsband.com
http://www.IZstyle.com

RESOURCES
http://www.dmbalmanac.com
http://www.dmbsetlist.com
http://www.dmbdate.com
http://www.songmeanings.net/artist.php?aid=43
http://www.dmbdiscography.com
Cali's Fabulous DMB Cookies!!
http://www.myspace.com/cali_matthews, calimatthews@hctmail.com

MEDIA
http://www.dmbvideos.com
http://www.dmbtabs.com
http://www.dmbdvds.com
http://www.dmbtattoo.com
http://www.dmbontv.com

http://www.wdmbradio.com
http://www.blogthatjanelikes.com
http://www.dancingfire.net
http://www.seekup.org

TORRENT SITES
http://www.dreamingtree.org
http://bt.etree.org
http://www.archive.org
http://www.thetradersden.org/index.php

WALLPAPER/ART
http://www.dmbwallpaper.net
http://www.driveindriveout.net
http://www.ljmsart.com
http://pablofineart.com/dmb/
http://www.errnine.com/links.html

COVER BANDS

Crash	http://www.aboutcrash.com
Ben Pezzner	http://www.benpezzner.com
Busted Stuff	http://www.bustedstuffband.com
Crowded Streets	http://www.crowdedstreetsband.com
Joe Busted Band	http://www.joebustedband.it
One Sweet World	http://www.onesweetworld.net/main
Rhyme and Reason	http://www.robmessina.com
	http://www.myspace.com/rhymeandreasonnj
Stepping Feet	http://www.steppingfeet.com/site8.aspx
Trippin Billies	http://www.trippinbillies.com/

TRADER SITES
http://db.etree.org
http://dmbshnhaven.net
http://www.dmbexchange.com

http://www.myspace.com/boydtinsleyspace
http://www.myspace.com/davematthewsband
http://www.myspace.com/trumpethornz
http://www.myspace.com/lowendude

Please check out this fabulous group of people with a great idea!

http://www.myspace.com/tailgateforacause
Be the change you want to see!

Since I began my website, I have been overwhelmed by the spirit of kindness and generosity that has been shown me.

Thank you for letting my mind see what my heart knew...that the influence of good will always win.
Maybe not everyday but many days...and that we each have dreams that need and thrive on encouragement...love...joy

My sincere thanks first to Dave whose brilliance and exploration into this journey called "life" has inspired me to take my own little trip. And to Carter, Boyd, Leroi, Stefan, Rashawn and Butch for taking those notes and chords and clefs and not only giving them life but then blasting them into the universe like some fairy dust that spreads life, love, joy to all it falls on.

Also to all the fans of the Dave Matthews Band who always lift me up with their kind words and inspirational stories...each and every day.

Special thanks to Tawny Richards, Mary Warner, Ceason Middleton, Becca Reaves, David Lago-Gonzalez, Kevin Coffee, Rick Harrington, my sweet Olivia, and my sister Jenni. My heart know no limits when it comes to my dear brother-in-law Robert and his most lovely Song Rong. Their perseverance and hard work are what has allowed this book to be. And to Dan Kunkemoeller whose patience and knowledge were so important to the process. I am so grateful.

So many thanks to all my "friends" on myspace for the continual encouragemen and invaluable help. What a network! You are all the greatest!

And if you know me, you know where my heart always lies and where my gratitude is boundless...
to my son and my husband.

My son for the inspiration from day one to be the best I could be
and my husband for always bringing the umbrella.
You are my heart...

"Don't lose the dreams inside your head"!!

about the author

Lynda Sokolowski was born...

Oh, do I have to do this part? Mary said, "People will want to know," There is not much to know...I was born in Marquette, Michigan, spent my childhood bopping around to wherever my Navy pilot Dad was sent. That meant Florida, California, Hawaii, Illinois and Pennsylvania. I was not the levelheaded woman that you now see before you. I was an artsy kid who loved Tim Buckley, the Mothers of Invention, the Grateful Dead and the Beatles. (All thanks by the way to my older boyfriend who I thought was the hippest thing ever. Asshole stood me up for the prom and I had to go with my neighbor's nephew! But that's a different book!)

i ended up at Drexel University in Philadelphia as a fashion design major but never quite clicked with the whole "fashion" thing. Got married very young and was "railroaded" by life, love and motherhood. I was going to say "held hostage" but that is not true. I love being a mother and my husband and children are my greatest gifts.

I experimented with several businesses in the nineties but never really found what made my heart sing...until that fateful day in the car. (See "Forward") And here I am! Living in Upstate New York in an old brick house where turkeys visit daily - painting, gardening, cooking, drinking wine, listening to DMB, loving my family (including my new little grandson!) and dreaming of new things that are right around the corner!

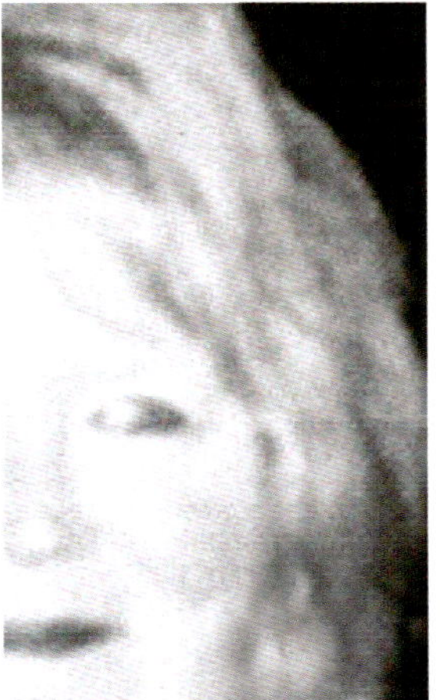

credits

Every effort has been made to be accurate and inclusive in regard to the credits. Since many of the photos have come as a result of a fan submission (sometimes only with a first name!), the author invites readers to notify her of any omissions or corrections. Many thanks to the beautiful people who shared their memories!

WAREHOUSE
Tiffany Gilkey, Bill Frakes/Sports Illustrated, David Adam Beloff, D'Ann, Tawny Richards, Jenn Berry, Reid Ladew, Paul Macca, Caitlin Kucharek, Meg Moore, Chelsea Bland, Amy Chagnon, Mase, Ben Sokolowski, Jesse DeVries, Jeremy Cannon, Heather Sokolowski

BUTTERFLY
Nadine Winn, David Adam Beloff, TripLight Imaging, Sam Kania, Jen, Artie Geminigio, Becca Reaves, Danelle Juline

DANCING NANCIES
Steve Speeney, Sara Suvada. David Adam Beloff, Cody Kruse. Laurie Lehner, Dayse Govea, Ben Sokolowski, Jeffrey Kanner. Erika Kabilian, Justin Falk

GRACE IS GONE
Michael Strohecker, Lynda Sokolowski, Dayse Govea, David Adam Beloff, Jenn Maroney

AMERICAN BABY
Derek Goff, Brad Grier, David Adam Beloff, Ben Sokolowski Eli Hartnett, Morgan Terry, Truman Purdy, Spencer Dyson

CRUSH
Justin Falk, David Adam Beloff

I'LL BACK YOU UP
Morgan Terry, Chelley Fierro-Andres, Casey McCarthy, Dayse Govea, Misty Kuhn, Ceason Middleton, Justin Falk, Gregg Ford, Amy Chagnon, Krystal Owen, Jan Navarro, Kelly Tobin, Valerie Shatford, Brenda Conto, Jennifer Balcom, David Adam Beloff

DREAMGIRL
Justin Falk, Ben Sokolowski, Chelsea Sanderson, Trish Holthausen, Rachel Bisom, Annie and Clem Smith, Zoey Heisey Kristy O'Connor, JJ, Kristi V, Jessica Porterfield, Katie Thaxton, Stephanie Morgan, Meg Moore, Stacy, Jennifer, Satu, Melinda Gorumba, Michelle Pando, Edith Leon, Stacie Deprey, Erika Kabilian, Sara Jane Ebel, Shelbe Roberts, Ashley, Amanda, Cari Western, Kasey Crall, Daniela M. Reagan, Mandi Andes, Gregg Ford, Cami, Dayse Govea, Misty Kuhn, Mary Mizen-Bruce, Sarah Henning, Danelle Juline, Chantel Laughlin, Wendi Stover, Nancy Black, Kimberly Bergan, Monica Green, Renae Kiley, Monica Green, Laura Unsworth, Terri Bland, Lori Rice, Cathy Velte, Calli, Ceason Middleton, Kira Zawacki, Laurie Lehner, Jon Coley, Becca Reaves, Rick Grobart, Kim Earley, Yolie Garcia, Kristy Thibodeau, Ben Sokolowski, Michelle Pando, David Adam Beloff

BARTENDER
Jenn Berry, Jason Wagner, Stacy, Lori Rice, David Adam Beloff, Kevin Coffee, Steve Speeney

TWO STEP
David Adam Beloff, Rachael ??, Tawny Richards, Ben Sokolowski, Dayse Govea, Jenn Berry, Heather Sokolowski, Samantha Stone, Rebecca Charros, Ben Sokolowski, Amy Chagnon, Mandi Andes, Rick Harrington, Cali Matthews

THE DAVE-NCI CODE
GIO

David Adam Beloff	Photography	www.davidadam.net email: davidadam@cox.net
David Lago-Gonzalez	Poet/Writer Most Extraordinary	http://www.myspace.com/con2o3elegancias
DMB Tattoo		http://www.myspace.com/dmbtattoo http://www.myspace.com/dmbtattoo
Kevin Coffee	Illustration/Cartooning	http://www.coffeespill.com/ http://www.myspace.com/coffeekev
GIO	Illustration/Manga	http://www.myspace.com/RingKingKaimirah
TripLight Imaging	Graphic Design	www.myspace.com/triplight
Wagner Photography	Photography	www.myspace.com/wagnerphotography